NO WAY OUT

THE WAR STORY OF A WWII BLACK BUFFALO SOLDIER

MW01290811

ROTHACKER SMITH

Copyright © 2009 Rothacker Smith
All rights reserved.

ISBN: 1-4392-5532-6
EAN13: 9781439255322

Visit www.booksurge.com to order additional copies.

NO WAY OUT

THE WAR STORY OF A WWII BLACK BUFFALO SOLDIER

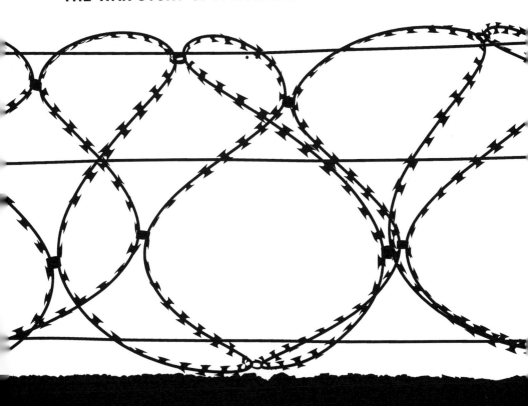

ROTHACKER SMITH

CONTENTS

PART IV AMERICAN LIBERATION

DEDICATION

I dedicate this book to the loving wife that God has given me, for her patient endurance of the trials and troubles I have brought into our lives. She has helped me to develop into a man—civilized, refined, and almost polished, "after the similitude of a palace."
I dedicate this book to Dorothy Louise Malson Smith.

• • •

ACKNOWLEDGMENTS:

I wish to acknowledge the help and assistance given to me in putting this book together. Kina Hinson, professor of English at Oakwood University in Huntsville, Alabama, for her very necessary assistance to give the story form and fashion. Bill Cleveland for his helpful suggestions toward the publication, and Barry Smith for his photography. I also received much encouragement and helpful suggestions from Jason McCracken, Elder C. D. Brooks, my wife and my children, and many others.

• • •

EDITOR'S NOTE TO THE READERS

The account set before you is true. This work chronicles the life of Professor Rothacker Childs Smith, Jr., from his boyhood days through his wartime realities on a World War II battlefront. Much of what you will find on these pages is a type of shorthand—each experience (and many others that remain unwritten) would take much more time and space to fully exhaust. Each time we discussed the manuscript, Dr. Smith's eyes took on a faraway look as he remembered, and then described in detail what he lived through. He is a kind, soft-spoken, Seventh-day Adventist Christian scholar and gentleman—who lived to tell about God's providence and protection through the horrors of World War II. Hence, this warning. This is *not* a book for children, even though the chapters are presented in brief, easy-to-read segments. The opening chapters recount an idyllic, Tom Sawyer-like boyhood, suitable for young listeners—if parents and other responsible adults choose to read to them. However, the chapters that follow, covering Dr. Smith's early days in the U.S. Army, his confrontations with racism in segregated "Jim Crow" America, religious bigotry among his own black commanding officers, and the conditions he endured as a soldier in transport, in Italian and German camps, and as a prisoner of war in German custody, are rough, raw, and graphic. They all took a heavy, personal toll. His accounts are plain, unadorned, and with disturbing imagery. He is also honest about the exploits of some fellow soldiers and the price of their immorality. As such, this story is not for the faint of heart, even among adults. Dr. Smith himself put it this way—it took a long time after his safe return home to become "civilized" again.

Think of David's wartime exploits found in God's Holy Word. Even though the chronicles are recorded plainly and honestly for the benefit of humanity, caution and discretion is exercised in exposing them to children. We pray God will bless the readers who plunge into these pages, and that He will make it easy to trace His hand in guiding the dangerous passage of a Christian young man through the perils of war. Kina Hinson

. . .

PART I – FAMILY HISTORY AND BOYHOOD DAYS

CHAPTER 1
The Story Begins

My story really began with an eleven-year-old boy, my grandfather. He left home and changed his name to Nelson Rodgers Smith. He hated his father—who had owned his mother. Years later, Grandfather married a woman whose mother had been a slave. My father was the middle child of the ten born to this couple. He was born on December 1, 1899.

My father. Rothacker Childs Smith Sr..entered Union College in Lincoln, Nebraska in 1916. He was the first to get a college degree. He began his professional career as a teacher in Harlem Academy in Harlem, New York in 1921 and became a colleague of James L Moran and Arna Bontemps. He later married Pearl Stephenson and I was their firstborn son, June 10, 1923. Three sons completed this family, Rothacker Childs Smith, Jr., Nelson Rodgers Smith, and Reger Cutting Smith. In September 1923, the family moved to a school located at Quaker Bridge, New York, and then to Conneaut, Ohio, where my two brothers were born. We had to return to New York City when my youngest brother was a few weeks old, because my mother had an aortic aneurysm. My mother died in early 1927 when my youngest brother was five months old.

In 1929, we were located in a farmhouse on a 160-acre farm near Medford, Long Island. This became the nucleus of a black community known today as Gordon Heights, New York. I integrated a seventy-five-year-old, one-room, first grade, schoolhouse in 1930, in Medford, Long Island. In 1932 we moved to Detroit, and in that same year, my father married his housekeeper, Mahala Williams, who became the loving mother who raised us. From 1934 to 1939, we lived in a large brick house (twenty-one rooms) with a large yard and a two-story barn in the back. Our address in those years was 3740 Bellevue. Sometime later, our old residence was torn down and the headquarters of the Pfeiffer Brewing Company was built on the spot. After those years, we had to get used to seeing our old address all over the city on their beer trucks.

. . .

CHAPTER 2
Inventions and Enterprises

During my growing-up years in Detroit, our father developed many strategies to keep his three sons occupied and busy with meaningful activities, especially during the summer months.

We helped him do landscaping work. He built a very sturdy three-wheeled wagon. The two rear wheels were cast iron. The handle was adapted from an old-fashioned push lawn mower. We used this wagon to collect anything that had any value. For instance, we collected coke from the ashes of coal-burning furnaces. When the nearby railroad line decided to change cross ties, we hauled used cross ties until we had over two hundred of them stacked in our yard. This provided the major source of fuel for at least one winter. They also provided resourceful play activities for the neighborhood children and us. Once we built a fort that was strong enough to climb on. We used bungs from the beer barrels of the brewery across the street as the ammunition. In the wintertime, we would use snowballs. Beer bungs are wooden plugs, shaped very much like a hockey puck. We had some glorious battles that often ended with a few minor wounds and one or two broken windows. Another time a tank car from the railroad line located a half a block from our house, sprang a leak and a nearby vacant lot ended up with a small lake of crude oil. We hauled crude oil home in 55 gal. drums. That winter we had an oil-fired furnace with a self invented burner. We brought home any piece of scrap iron or other metal that we found in our wanderings. When we had to move in 1939, we were able to sell over 1,400 lbs. of scrap iron alone. We used to make protose (an imitation meat) and sell it to some of the church members. We made bars of soap that had no lard in them, which we also sold to some of the church members. We also bought day-old baby chicks, raised them, and sold them. One project, which took a lot of work and energy, was the construction of a mouse circus. This device worked as an advertising gimmick for storefronts or in shop windows. We had to catch live field mice because house mice were too lazy! The mice would climb up on various wheels or merry-go-rounds and run for hours. We put our first one in the window of an Adventist brother's barbershop. The mice attracted so much attention that the sidewalk became crowded and the crowd expanded into the street. The police required us to remove the mouse circus. The experience with the mouse circus taught us a whole lot about the biology of mice. We had to construct a mouse maternity hospital. We found that the mice would get lazy after a while and so we would have to catch new ones. That didn't solve the problem because the old ones would fight the new ones until one or the other was destroyed. So we abandoned that industry.

The industrial project that lasted the longest was the sale of root beer. We made root beer and bottled it in discarded 12 oz. beer bottles, which were very plentiful because of the Eighteenth Amendment. With 5 gal. of root beer, we could fill fifty bottles. The yeast in the root beer would grow and produce carbon dioxide. It would take three days of incubation to make the root beer effervesce like any other soda pop. We sold this root beer for 3¢ a bottle. The first two summers in the root beer business, we would sell fifty bottles a day. We took the doors off an old refrigerator and laid it on its back on our wagon. We packed root beer in one compartment with at least 25 lb. of ice.

For our third summer, Dad acquired an old horse-drawn milk wagon. He painted in bold letters on the sides, **SMITH BROTHERS ROOT BEER, 3¢ a bottle.** Each day we sold three hundred bottles of root beer. I would leave home at about seven in the morning to go to a livery stable and rent a horse and wagon. ($2 a day). I would drive to the house on Bellevue, unhitch the horse from the livery wagon, and hitch him to the root beer wagon. By this time, my brothers would have loaded the wagon with the three hundred bottles in a tank with 50 lb. of ice. Some days we would take fifteen or twenty fried fish sandwiches to sell. Then we had to drive out to the city limits where project houses were being built. We would arrive about ten o'clock and sell our root beer until about one thirty or two. There were many vacant fields adjacent to the building site. We would tether the horse and let him graze (I was driving a gelding) until we were ready to go home. We had to drive home, hitch the horse back to the livery wagon, return him to the stable, and get back home on the streetcar. Then I would help my brothers with the remaining tasks required to have three hundred bottles ready for the next day's sale.

Driving the horse that summer made me think of a story that my father told us that happened to him when he was my same age, fourteen. A horse that pulled a wagon was harnessed between two wooden shafts. The wagons I drove were no exception. Dad was driving the horse in the driveway beside his house in Denver. There was a strip of grass on the other side of the driveway and then a fence. Another horse was tied to the fence and it was eating the grass near the driveway. The horse that Dad was driving kept veering toward that same strip of grass so that he could get a bite or two on his way to the barn. This caused the shaft on that side to enter the rear end of the other horse in the exact orifice designed for the elimination of second hand food. By the time Dad came to his senses, the shaft had penetrated about fourteen or fifteen inches into the horse's backside. Dad pulled back on the reins, hollered "whoa" and then "back." The rear end of the penetrated horse was in an agitated circular motion as though responding to the beat of some fast dance music. The shaft was finally backed out and as soon as the end emerged, a cloud of horse dobs erupted. Subsequently, no sign of injury appeared to have resulted from the penetration.

I do remember driving the horse one day on the way home with the root beer wagon during a thunderstorm, when a bolt of lightning struck the pavement about three feet from the horse's head. It seemed as though a fiery white telephone pole suddenly struck the pavement. The horse didn't seem to flinch and neither did I. Two or three days before the summer ended in my fourteenth year, the year of the horse, on our way home with the root beer wagon, I was stopped by a cop who demanded to see my license. He then informed me that I could not legally drive a horse until I was sixteen and had a driver's license. That ended our root beer enterprise.

Some of my activities during the next two years included selling a straightening comb that my grandfather had developed. I had a bicycle and I visited most of the black beauty shops on Detroit's lower east side. Grandfather had developed a straightening comb that was more durable and less subject to looseness than any competitors. I sold these to the beauty shops and picked up their combs that needed repairing and cleaning. Grandfather would straighten the teeth and clean them so that they looked like new again.

I also spent some time working in a variety store. In the seven months that I worked for Rivkin's Variety Store, my wages increased from 5¢ an hour to 12¢ an hour. I enjoyed the challenges and the variety of that job. I remember a mother who purchased a tricycle and asked me to wrap it. I took a short strip of brown paper, wrapped it around one handlebar, and tied it with a piece of string. My boss was so pleased because he thought that I was going to use an awful lot of paper trying to wrap up a whole tricycle.

· · ·

CHAPTER 3
The Old Model A Ford

One of my uncles was driving his Model A Ford coupe on a busy multilane street when he pulled the steering wheel off the steering shaft in his car. He managed to get the car to the curb with the aid of a pair of pliers. He was so disgusted with that car that he gave it to me with the proviso that he never had to see it again. He sold it to me for $1 so that I could obtain a legal title. I still have that title. When I would go to visit him I would park on the next street and walk around the block to his house. I drove that car for seven years. Its windshield wiper, as was the custom in those days, relied on engine vacuum to work. The wiper was very fast when going downhill and would stop completely when going uphill. My brother and I solved the uphill problem by using two pieces of string. He would pull the wiper blade toward his side and I would pull it back.

One could look down through the floorboards and see the pavement passing underneath. In cold weather, a single drop of water would freeze in the fuel system and act as a ball check valve, shutting down the engine without warning. Sometimes a vigorous shake would dislodge the ice ball and the car would start and run again. Other times it would not start until the temperature rose above freezing. In Detroit, that would often be two or three weeks, which meant that we would ride the street railway system, where the fare was 6¢ and a transfer was a penny. I washed that car only twice during the seven years that I owned it because it looked the same after washing as before. I averaged thirty miles to a flat. When a tire went flat, I could stop the car, jack it up, remove the wheel, dismount the tire, patch the inner tube, remount the tire, remount the wheel, pump the tire up to pressure, and be on my way again in fifteen minutes.

More than once, I would have a quarter, 25¢. I could take my girl-friend out for a ride. I would buy a gallon of gas, get two double-dip ice-cream cones, and have 5¢ left when I got home. Gas was 10¢ per gallon and ice cream cones were two dips for a nickel.

• • •

CHAPTER 4
I Leave Home – Off to College and World War II Begins

I graduated in January 1941 from Northern High School in Detroit. I matriculated in Emmanuel Missionary College in Berrien Springs, Michigan in September 1941. My major was agriculture, and my minor was biology. At that time, there were six African American dormitory students. EMC during those years enhanced our social development by limiting our dining room seating to black-only tables. If one of the off-campus African American students chose to eat in the cafeteria for a particular meal, someone would have to sit at a table by himself. Since I worked on the farm and sometimes arrived late, I often enjoyed my meal in solitary splendor while all the tables around me were filled with a regular component of six students each.

I remember listening to the radio in English 101 on December 8, 1941, when Franklin Delano Roosevelt spoke those words that put us into World War II.

The campus changed very little for the rest of the 1941–42 school year. I was baptized into the Seventh-day Adventist Church in January 1942. I had been attending the church in South Bend, Indiana, but its pastor there was an intern. And so we made a trip to Indianapolis, where Elder Lawrence, one of our stalwart pioneer ministers, baptized me. When the spring semester ended, I returned to Detroit to try to recoup my finances. I passed a civil service exam from the city of Detroit, and became the first African American forestry helper in the city of Detroit. I really enjoyed the work and I gained some skills that I used many times in later life. I was making the princely sum of $.90 per hour. Laborers at Ford Motor Company made only $1.35 an hour that year.

• • •

PART II – IN THE ARMY NOW

CHAPTER 5
Greetings from Uncle Sam

In January 1943, I received one of those letters whose salutation was, "Greetings, your friends and neighbors..." I was soon classified IA-0, which meant that I was fit for duty and that I was a conscientious objector. I reported for duty at the train station in Detroit on Monday, March 1, 1943. By Wednesday at 4:30 a.m., I had arrived at Camp Custer, near Battle Creek, Michigan, received new clothes, been injected in both arms, begun my introduction to army protocol, and reported for KP. It was below zero outside and the mess sergeant ordered me to mop the wooden boards that made up the walkway to the mess hall. I told the sergeant that it was too cold to mop, but he, with the use of a few choice four-letter words, ordered me to mop the walk. So I took a mop and a bucket of hot water and proceeded to coat the boards with ice. Later, I had the distinct pleasure of seeing the sergeant slip on the ice and almost break his neck. I carefully hid from him my mirth and enjoyment of his predicament.

On Thursday, sixteen of us were ordered to ship out that evening. We boarded a train, under the command of a corporal and were bound for somewhere south. When we got to Cincinnati, we began to realize what Jim Crow really meant. We sixteen were from Detroit, Chicago, and two from Bay City, Michigan. We had to get out of the comfortable coach in which we began our journey, and board the coach right behind the coal-burning steam engine. We finally arrived in Camp Stewart, Georgia, where the sixteen of us became the medical detachment for the 492nd antiaircraft battalion. The sixteen of us were from up North while the other nearly nine hundred were all southerners. Some of the cadre told us that we northerners would have problems because we did not know how to act under Jim Crow. Six months later, the same sergeant told us that we were better behaved than many of the others.

· · ·

CHAPTER 6
Medic Training – and Other Adventures

We did "on the job training," as medics. I had to give a brother a shot in his hip. I was scared and nervous and he tightened his muscles just when I tried to inject the needle. The needle instead plowed a furrow across both cheeks. I then ducked in time to miss the blow when he swung at me. I soon learned how to give shots and later became an expert.

Our commanding officer, a doctor, was a second lieutenant who favored me. He told me that he had looked up the Army General Classification Test scores and that I had the highest score in the battalion. He chose me to be his driver and issued me the keys to a brand new jeep. I was in heaven. After taps one night, our cadre corporal awakened me from sleep and persuaded me that we could go riding in the jeep without getting into trouble. He didn't have to persuade very hard. And so we would go out riding, putting the jeep through its paces. We drove through ditches, jumping off low embankments, through mud puddles, etc. We would wash the jeep, park it in its place and go back to bed. Sometime during the second week, while I was driving, the CO examined the official trip log. On paper, we had driven fifteen miles. The odometer read better than fifteen hundred miles. The doctor exclaimed that we would bankrupt the army, so he turned the jeep in and got a big ungainly ambulance. Needless to say, there was no romance to driving the ambulance during the night. I did no more unauthorized night driving.

At the end of the second month, I received one stripe. I was a Pfc. I soon learned that Pfc meant "praying for corporal." A little later, two of us received orders to report to school at the William Beaumont General Hospital in El Paso, Texas, for the surgical technician course. This was an eight-week course.

One Sabbath, in El Paso, I was welcomed to worship in the white Seventh-day Adventist Church. There was no black Adventist Church in El Paso at that time. This caused some grief from some of the EMC Adventists I ran into at church, who had been my schoolmates. That afternoon after church, three white brothers decided that their appetite for some ice cream became an "ox in the mire" situation, so the four of us entered a little ice cream shop. I did not plan to buy anything. But the four of us sat down on stools and they began to give their orders. There was a young woman behind the cash register who kept tapping her teeth with the end of a pencil. She said to one of the others that they did not serve colored. I knew what she had said and so I said I was not going to eat or to order anything. Then she asked me if I would rather wait outside, I replied no, I was comfortable so I would wait where I was sitting. Then she asked me if I would wait outside. I had just started to get up when some man in overalls said to me, "You heard the lady, now get out." I looked at him and asked him if he was the chief bouncer. Then he said to me, "No more sass out of you." I told him that I was a Pfc. in the army and he was still a civilian; therefore, he was sassing me. I walked back to the camp in hot anger on that Sabbath day.

When we returned to Georgia, we met the immediate aftermath of a riot that had taken place in our absence. An antiaircraft outfit of African American veteran soldiers was relocated to Camp Stewart from the Michigan-Canadian border. Some of them had French-Canadian wives. At least two of these had come to visit their husbands in Georgia. One Saturday afternoon, an African American sergeant with his white wife attempted to board the bus for the trip to town (Savannah). They were attacked and beaten to death. He died that day, his wife died the next day. His unit was composed of two- to three-year veterans who did not take this atrocity lying down. This outfit took over the main gate so that for three days no one could enter or leave. Some white people, civilians as well as military, were killed. We never knew how many. We got back from Texas to an uneasy peace. It wasn't long before the repercussions began. One African American battalion, not the veteran battalion, was singled out for punishment. Two noncoms were sentenced to ten to twenty-five years of hard labor. All of the noncoms in the battalion were busted to private. The whole battalion, which had finished the eighteen weeks of training, was set back to the sixth week of training. Then a directive came down from the War Department in Washington stating that African American troops were mentally incompetent to learn to fire antiaircraft weapons. This after our battalion had the best training record on the post, including black and white. We had gone through the eighteen weeks of training with no setbacks. Normally an outfit would go through three or four weeks of training and take a test. If the soldiers passed the test, the next phase of training would begin. If the test was unsatisfactory, the unit would be set back to the last test and go through that training again. Most battalions required twenty to thirty weeks to complete the eighteen weeks of training.

Secret orders and instructions were issued to the officers of the various units of the battalion. Our CO left his orders on his desk and I got to read the copy sent to our medical detachment. Among the things that he was to tell us: We were once slaves who were owned by Christian masters who loved us so much that they set us free. Therefore, we should be thankful to them and respect them. We should get off the sidewalk and respectfully let them pass. We should always address them as "sir." There were other instructions in that each officer was to find a willing soldier who would report to him the things that soldiers discussed in the barracks at night.

Our basic training had continued during the eighteen weeks. Our cadre sergeant wisely scheduled a twenty-mile hike three times a week. So we would hike away from our barracks compound down the road toward the forest. When we got to the first clump of trees, we would disperse and find comfortable spots, stretch out, and snooze the afternoon away.

One afternoon, a few of us were assigned as medics to accompany a company on a real twenty-mile hike. I ended up as the medic who had to take care of the blisters that developed on the feet of the marchers. That is how I learned that unwashed feet in the climate of a South Georgia summer have an odor that is almost sickening. I had to take those feet in my hands, puncture and bandage the blisters, and then tag them to wait for an ambulance.

A few days later, I found myself in a boxcar with about twenty other men bound for Texas. We had an eight-hour layover in Birmingham. Two of the guys had gotten permission to visit family or friends in Birmingham via the local streetcar system. On streetcars in the South, each seat had a bracket that held a little two-sided sign that had "colored" on one side and "white" on the other. The colored side faced the rear and colored people had to sit so that they faced the colored side. In most cities, the signs could be moved forward if most of the passengers were African American or back if most of the passengers were white. In Birmingham, that sign could not be moved past the middle seat no matter what the passenger load indicated. These two guys moved the sign one seat ahead of the middle seat. The streetcar stopped, the cops were called, and they were arrested. Our train ride was held up until the next day.

When I arrived in Texas, I found myself in a quartermaster company whose TO (table of organization) called for 110 men and fifty-five 6 × 6 trucks. We were classified as so mentally deficient that we had white medics and white clerk-typists. Each of us was either a truck driver or an assistant truck driver. Some of the assistant drivers were assigned as cooks to staff our mess hall. That was a very low day for me. I was a corporal, had a surgical technician MOS (military occupational specialty), and now the United States of America had officially pronounced me as mentally incompetent to be a medic. Since I already had a military driver's license, I was assigned as a truck driver and usually as the last truck in a convoy. I don't remember ever having an assistant driver. I have enjoyed driving all of my life. When we started the phase of our training on the highway, I enjoyed being the tail end of the convoy. I was now a five-month veteran with T-5 (technician fifth grade) stripes. I was able to visit an outfit on the post that was a training company for new recruits. I met the second lieutenant who was the CO (commanding officer) of that company, and he let me visit my brother Nelson who was a three-week recruit. We were able to go to town on Sabbath where forty or fifty Adventists worshiped each week. There I met several guys that I would later meet again at Oakwood College.

One afternoon our convoy was ordered to drive about twenty miles to a large area that had widely spaced short trees. We were ordered to disperse the trucks and camouflage them with tree limbs. The trees were just about as tall as the trucks. We had supper in the area and after dark, we were ordered to form the convoy and proceed out to the highway using blackout lights. It was decided to test the wrecker dispersal system by leaving a "disabled" truck in the bivouac area. My truck was chosen to be disabled by using a screwdriver to poke a hole in one of the front blackout lenses. A special ticket was attached to my truck and I was instructed to wait until a wrecker came. I watched and listened until the convoy disappeared and then the sounds faded from my hearing. I then turned on my headlights and followed the tracks out of the woods to the highway. I headed back to camp at full speed and entered the motor pool right behind the last truck. I expected to be brought up on charges the next day, but I never heard another word about it.

After two months, I was transferred out to another quartermaster outfit in Texas, but this time I was assigned as a medic. Here I was also able to go to church almost very Sabbath. I was stationed at Camp Howze, Texas. Camp Howze was located in the Texas panhandle just six miles from the Oklahoma border. I would alternate between Oklahoma City and Dallas, the locations of the nearest African American churches. In either case, the first part of my journey would be by train. The local rail line was the Atchison, Topeka, and the Santa Fe. There was a popular song on the radio that sang, "The folks around here get the time of day from the Atchison, Topeka, and the Santa Fe." I once caught a train that was twenty-three hours, forty-five minutes late. It was really fifteen minutes early for the next day.

There was no African American Adventist church in Fort Worth in 1943. I would ride the train to Fort Worth and catch a bus to Dallas. One Sabbath after church, I boarded a crowded bus bound for Fort Worth. There was standing room only and I was the only African American passenger. So I made my way as far toward the back of the bus as I could. A bench seat extended across the back and so I stood holding on to a post near the back. The bus had traveled some distance, when the driver stopped the bus and came to the back and ordered me to come up to the front and stand by him until the back was empty. I told him I thought I was supposed to go to the back. I was addressed as "nigger" during this conversation. I was really angry. I had a switchblade knife in my pocket. My mother had received it as a souvenir from Florida, and I had secretly borrowed it the last time I was home. I debated in my mind as how to kill the bus driver and maybe one other person before I would be killed. I decided to live, burning with anger, because there was nothing I could do about it. As we traveled, more and more people got off until there was an empty space on the rear bench. I went to the back and sat in the empty seat between white passengers. In a little while, the driver missed me. He stopped the bus, vociferously came to the back, and ordered me to stand by him until the whole back bench was empty. This time the debate in my mind was fierce and lasted for some miles. My anger so consumed me that when I got back to camp I did not speak to anyone for several hours.

On Thanksgiving Day, 1943, Joe Louis visited our camp, our company, and ate dinner in our mess hall, at my table. I was eight places away from him. After dinner, he asked the captain if he could use the telephone to call his wife. I was asked to escort him to the office where the phone was located. I had a brief conversation with the boxing heavy weight champion of the world on the way to make that phone call.

One night our company was ordered to bivouac in the fields. I walked out as an aid man with the company and, after sunset, it was a very pleasant hike because of the full moon. When we were about two to three miles from camp, somebody got sick and I was ordered to run back to camp and get a jeep. On my way back, the sandy dirt road wound through a wide grassy meadow. It seemed as though a hay crop had been harvested within the past month. As I started through the field, I noticed hundreds of rabbits having a dance. They were hoping up and down, sometimes two or four in unison, and sometimes one would go up while his partner would go down. They were spread all across the field and even in the road, absorbed in dancing. Those in the road would move just enough so that I would not run over them but they seemed otherwise oblivious to my presence. When I had passed through them, I continued on my mission. When I returned, riding in the back of the jeep, the sudden appearance of the jeep with its headlights on broke the spell and the rabbits scattered in all directions. I have read since, that rabbit dances often occur on the night of a full moon. In some cases, their natural predators can walk into the edge of the dance and grab a victim, kill him, and then return to the dance for another. These "uninvited guests" to the dance would include foxes and bobcats.

Soon after Thanksgiving, I was shipped out to join the Ninety-second Division stationed in Fort Huachuca, Arizona. This time my stay was less than a month. Before this and after this posting, I learned to expect to be posted to a new location or to a different outfit every two months. Right after Christmas, I was posted to Camp Atterbury, Indiana. I was assigned to the Second Battalion Medical Section of the 366th Infantry Regiment. An infantry regiment has about three thousand men. Each infantry division was made up of three infantry regiments and other supporting components for a total of fourteen thousand or more soldiers. Seven African American infantry regiments were activated during WW II. Three of these were assigned to the Ninety-second Division and three to the Ninety-third Division. Our regiment was separate and unique in that it had no white officers. It was the War Department's official policy to assign white officers to African American troops. And since most African Americans were from the South, the southern white man was thought best able to "control" them. It was in Fort Huachuca that I took my first real twenty-mile hike. I remember struggling to a certain checkpoint just ahead of a certain lieutenant. An announcement the next day said that all those who came in behind that lieutenant had to do the hike over again the next Saturday.

In Huachuca, on Christmas Day, we did not have to fall out to make any formation and we enjoyed a special Christmas dinner.

A few days later, I was posted from the Ninety-second Division to the 366th Infantry Regiment stationed much nearer to home in camp Atterbury, Indiana. The 366th was all African American from our bird colonel commanding officer down. The regiment was a political headache for the government. African American troops were deemed unfit for combat. This mandate did not change until two months after D day. We were the only all-black infantry regiment in WW II. Infantrymen are trained for combat. When I joined the regiment in January 1944, they had been stationed in Fort Devens, Massachusetts, for over two and a half years. They had then been posted to Camp A.P. Hill, Virginia, for three or four months. A.P. Hill was about five hours away by train from New York and since most of the 366th were from the eastern seaboard, many would head toward the big city on the weekend passes. When Saturday leave time came, they would go to the local train station and board any coach with an open door. They would spread out through the coaches and occupy any empty seat in spite of the gentle entreaties by the white conductors to board the colored coach. Another day a bunch of them went into town and removed all of the signs that said "colored" or "white." The local citizens petitioned the War Department to please remove them from their neighborhood. They had not been at Camp Atterbury, Indiana, very long when I arrived and joined the regiment. I was assigned as a medic in the Second Battalion medical section.

On my first Sabbath in Indiana, I reported to the company commander and requested permission to go to town so that I could attend church. I was told to doff my uniform and to help scrub the barracks so it would be ready for inspection. I asked permission to speak to the chaplain. The captain said, "There's the phone."

I talked to the chaplain, who happened to be a colonel, who then asked me to put the captain on the line. After their conversation the captain told me, "Go to church, buck private," as he reached up and tore the stripes off one sleeve of my overcoat. He added something about my being too young to have rank in that outfit. So I remained a buck private for the rest of my army career, thanks to a zealous African American officer. I often attended church in Indianapolis, and I even managed to go home to Detroit two or three times.

About the end of March, we shipped out to Newport News, Virginia, where we boarded a ship that, nine days later, landed us in Casablanca, North Africa. Our ship was not part of a convoy and so we followed a course with a lot of zigs and zags. Crossing the Atlantic on a ship was very pleasant, at first. We had to remain below deck at night in our tiered bunks. We seemed to get seasick faster below deck than we did topside. Often the man in the top bunk would upchuck over the side of his bunk on each of the four bunks below him. We had to stand in line in the hall and passageways for over three hours for each meal. It felt like being in an elevator that went from the first floor to the third floor without ever stopping to open the door. Just up and down, up and down until you were utterly miserable and yet hungry (you had emptied your last meal down the head long ago). We had to stand up to eat. We ate from metal compartmental trays that were on steel shelving almost chest high. Sometimes the ship would tilt and all the trays would slide to one end of the rails. We would go on eating out of whichever tray stopped in front of us until the opposite roll of the ship would send the trays in the other direction.

We disembarked in Casablanca, North Africa. The second day in Africa found us in boxcars bound from Casablanca to Oran. European boxcars are different from American boxcars. They have only four wheels. They are joined together by three giant chain links. Each car has two heavy spring-loaded plungers that keep a certain distance between each car and its neighbor. When the engine is pulling, the chins are stretched so that the cars are the maximum distance apart. When the engine slows, the chains slacken and the cars can come closer to each other until the plungers stop them. This distance may permit the inter car distance to vary by as much as two feet. And so we found ourselves in these thirty-two and eight boxcars. (thirty-two men or eight horses) Our ride was pleasant, the doors were open and we had plenty of blankets. Our food was cold C rations, which for me was cold canned meat and vegetable stew. This diet generated much constipation and crude conditions.

Sewage disposal meant stopping the train in remote areas so that we could endeavor to empty our bowels. In many cases, the body waste was so hard to eject that if one squatted too low, the downward movement would force the body upward. If the train whistle blew, and we had to return to the boxcars, we would simply reach down, break off what was exposed, and remain plugged with the rest until the next rest stop.

At one portion of the journey, I was in the end car. When the engine would stop, the cars that were the most distal would keep on rolling until all of the plungers had compressed their springs. Then the springs would expand and push the cars back. The end car would back up thirty or forty or more feet until all of the chains were stretched. The chains would pull the distal cars forward again until the plungers were compressed, but not as tightly as the first time. The end car would pass the same spot four or five times before coming to rest.

On the morning of the first day of our trip, a guy who was sick and hung-over from Casablanca wine upchucked on my blankets. I drew back my fist to hit him but my arm could not move forward. The guys explained to me that I could not hit him since I didn't drink. Only a drinker has the right to hit another drinker, according to them.

On the fourth day of our journey, we arrived at Oran, Africa. We were trucked about twenty-two miles from the city. We finally arrived at a level plane where we set up camp by pitching pup tents. We could walk a few hundred feet to the edge of a bluff that overlooked a wide valley. We could see two or three towns connected by the railway. We could watch the train make its way from town to town, starting and stopping and puffing out smoke in the process.

One night the powers that be decided to entertain us by showing a movie. The theatre was a nearby flat-bottomed ravine. The screen was a bed sheet stretched between two trees. The projector and the generator to power it were on the back of a 6 × 6. A few guys were on the back of the truck, the rest of us sat on the ground or stood up. The movie didn't start until after dark. In the middle of the picture, someone hollered "SNAKE." Panic and pandemonium broke loose. The guys on the truck were jumping off like popcorn. Those on the ground started running in every direction. I got into a semi squatting position because I decided that I needed to know which direction to run before I ran. Three or four people caromed off me. One looked like he turned a couple of cartwheels before he fell. I saw two guys run into each other head-on and both fell backward. At least one ran into me and fell backward. The next day I asked around and could find no one who had seen the snake.

We were about twenty-two miles from Oran. I got passes to Oran twice from this camp. Oran had the appearance of a European city. A part of the city was an Arab ghetto. The streets were very narrow and there were no sidewalks. The Arab ghetto was off-limits to all troops. White American soldiers and Arabs shared a genuine hatred for each other. White soldiers who got drunk and wandered into the ghetto were never again seen alive or identified. Two or three soldiers would be walking together noisily down one of the narrow streets. When passing a certain door, three hands would reach out. One would grab the mouth, the middle one would grab the belt, and the bottom one would grab an ankle. The whole man would suddenly and silently disappear. Oftentimes the soldiers would not even notice one was missing for a while. The next morning, several naked bodies would be found at the border of the ghetto. Their teeth would be smashed. Any birthmarks or tattoos would have been sliced off. The MPs would have the names of so many missing and they would attach a name to a body because they could not recognize anyone. The Arabs robbed the ones they captured because even if they had no money, jewelry, or watches, their uniform was worth more than $100 on the black market. A pair of cotton boxer shorts could sell for $7 or $8.

Back at our camp one afternoon, some of us were talking to a young Arab boy who suddenly took off running. When we looked up, we saw two white soldiers in a jeep driving about one hundred yards from us. When they saw the boy running they began to chase him with the jeep. When they got close enough, they stopped. One got out and shot the boy down as one would a fleeing rabbit. They then laughingly shook hands (high fives were not yet invented).

All combat troops on R & R in Oran were treated so badly by the local occupation command that problems occurred with combat rotations and replacements. Black troops were treated even worse. Our guys were treated so badly—having to pay fines for almost nonexistent infractions, getting beat with Billy clubs—that revenge became a major consideration. One of the guys in my outfit had a metal plate in his head. I could feel dents made in that plate by an MP's club the night before.

I was walking on the sidewalk on a street with many storefront shops. I passed behind a lieutenant who was bent over with his forehead against the window while he was studying the jewelry displayed there. Just before I passed his back, I looked across the street and saw two first lieutenants with MP armbands who were walking the beat as foot cops. I immediately saluted the shave tail's back. The two MPs nodded their heads to let me know that if I had not saluted they would have arrested me. The order is that one salutes an officer when an officer is approaching and can return the salute. You do not salute an officer's backside when he is unaware of your presence. The final insult came when our CO, a bird colonel, was denied entrance to the officer's club because he was black.

Our regiment decided to invade Oren and shoot up a few key locations such as the officer's club, the MP station, etc. Being infantry, we were armed. Most black outfits had whatever weapons had been issued to them, then stored as quartermaster supplies at headquarters. All of our ammunition was supposed to have been turned in to the quartermaster at headquarters. But the guys proceeded to find the rounds of ammo that had been hidden in various places, such as wrapped in paper in canteens.

A quartermaster transportation battalion was camped less than a half mile on our flank. We instructed the drivers to fully load their trucks with gas and to sleep soundly so they would not know who borrowed their trucks when the time came. The attack was scheduled for the next Thursday. On Wednesday, we were ordered to break camp and, by Wednesday night, we had boarded a ship in Oran harbor and sailed away from the coast of Africa before sunset, bound for Italy.

We watched the sun set on the beautiful Mediterranean Sea. The whole trip was very beautiful and pleasant. The bow waves produced myriads of phosphorescent lights along the sides of the ship.

This was a British ship with British crew and so we ate British food. It seemed as though all of their cooking was done in iron pots hanging over a fireplace. They cooked all of the food in the one pot. And they cooked each item on the menu in a cloth bag. All of the food seemed to have the same flavor, whether it was the beef stew or the pudding for dessert. I particularly remember eating a dessert whose name sounded like "blank mange" that had the distinctive flavor of sweetened beef stew. But we survived.

The next afternoon we arrived in Naples, Italy. The harbor had several sunken ships as well as active manned ships. Our ship docked beside a capsized ship and our gangplank ended on the side of the sunken vessel. We walked to a causeway that led to the side of another ship and finally to a causeway that led to shore. Our regiment was fragmented in Naples. I think that our Second Battalion medic section with some other elements of battalion headquarters pitched camp (pup tents) on a vacant lot in urban Naples. Our latrine was a slit trench parallel to the sidewalk and about two feet away from it. I waited until the third night trying to find privacy from the civilian foot traffic on the sidewalk. I was in the midst of the process in the squatting position when three women walked past. I later learned that Italians' ideas about modesty and privacy were very different from ours. I passed street urinals for men that were located in the walls of buildings on the edge of the sidewalk on busy downtown streets.

After about three days in Naples, our medical detachment relocated near Foggia. Our regiment was split up and assigned all over southern Italy. The Anzio beachhead was about one month old when we arrived in Italy in April 1944. Our mission was to provide air base security and to guard ammunition dumps, bomb dumps, etc. I would be assigned to different locations to provide medical support for the troops in their different guard duty assignments. From mid-April until late September, I lived in bast Italia, (base or bottom) sunny Italy, almost as on vacation. I was usually reassigned about every two months. Southern Italy was the territory of the Fifteenth Air Force. Two or three of my assignments were at plane landing strips. We often saw planes in the sky. Sometimes they staged mock dogfights. They did all kinds of stunts, such as flying under bridges, buzzing various ground sites, chasing or racing each other, etc.

In Foggia, we were near a B-17 bomber strip. These four-engine bombers had to fly four hours in friendly skies to break in a new engine before going on the next bombing mission. I would often visit their field and hitch a ride on the break-in missions. I had never been in a plane before and I greatly enjoyed those rides. The B-17s had a Plexiglas nose that one could sit in so that while in flight it seemed as though you were sitting in space and flying through space. On one trip, the pilot asked me if the neat rows of pup tents were my camp. Then he said, "Let's go down and have some fun." I got out of the nose before he buzzed our camp by flying down a line of pup tents about twelve feet off the ground. Two different tents suddenly developed a bulge and then rose up, ripping and pulling out the stakes, and took off running. Two or three of the brothers stood waving their fists and shouting some kind of blessings or the opposite of blessings. One brother who was squatting astraddle the slit trench latrine at the edge of camp tried to run from the squatting position but fell headlong beside the trench because his pants were down around his ankles. When that flight was over, I sneaked back to camp. I did get asked once, "Where were you when that plane flew over?"

My most enjoyable assignment was with a company guarding an ammunition dump near the Adriatic seaport of Manfredonia. I was the only medic attached to 134 men and officers. Our camp was pitched about three hundred yards from the shore. We were in squad tents by this time. Each tent could sleep eight. Our camp was located on a tableland that was about twenty feet above sea level. We had a private beach located in a cove that was about two or three hundred yards wide with an almost perfect sandy beach. The cove gave us privacy, which we needed because bathing suits were not part of our clothing issue. (During WW II, it was against the law for a soldier to wear civilian clothes at any time, even civilian pajamas in bed at night.) My duty was to hold sick call every morning, to see that the latrine was dug and maintained, and to see that proper hygiene was observed in the mess hall. After sick call, I was free until the next day. I spent a lot of time in town learning the language. I would take my GI breakfast and trade it to an Italian teenager for his piece of whole wheat bread with olive oil. I would go swimming almost every day when some of the off-duty guys were swimming. I found a discarded auxiliary gasoline tank from a fighter plane and I constructed a kayak from it. The tank is tear-shaped, about two and a half feet in diameter in the biggest part, and about six feet long. I cut two round holes and lined the cut edges with split hose to keep the metal from cutting us when we sat in the cockpits. The kayak was very unstable, and it would almost capsize if you breathed out of the wrong side of your nose. One day, while swimming, I saw an Italian fishing boat sailing parallel to the shore with a rope trailing behind it. I swam out, grabbed the rope, and let it pull me on my back for a very nice ride. When I let go, I thought that I was about fifty feet from shore. But I was so far that I could not see the shore. Treading water to get my bearings, I could see shore when the crest of a small wave would raise me up—then shore looked like a thin line in the distance. I had not told anybody that I was going for the ride, and so here I was out in the sea and nobody even knew that I was there. My life could have ended there and I would have been listed as missing in action unless my body washed up on shore. It took me more than an hour to get back to the beach.

On another day, six or seven of us were standing on the beach when we saw a sailfish swimming near the surface. The sail appeared above the surface, and then it became immersed until just a tip was visible. The fish swam across our view from right to left in this rhythmic leisurely fashion, oblivious to our presence. The guys produced two M-1 rifles, two Thompson submachine guns, and two .30-caliber carbines. They began to fire at the fish until the bullets made froth on the surface of the water around the sail. Some bullets actually ricocheted off the surface of the water. The fish never varied its course or style while we could see it. Afterward they counted the empty shell cases and found that they had fired over six thousand rounds.

I remember the sixth day of June 1944. I was reclining in the shade underneath a large tree, watching and counting over 860 planes form a huge circle in the sky as different squadrons and groups joined the circle. Then the whole force headed north toward southern Europe. It was D-day. Over four thousand men died on the beaches that day. Very few were black because the government had declared black troops unfit for combat. It wasn't until August that we were officially declared fit to enter into combat where we would be shooting at a white enemy.

I was later assigned to Second Battalion headquarters, located near a P-51 fighter group located near the town of San Severo. Here my assignment was as the ambulance driver. This ambulance was a Dodge 4 × 4 weapons carrier that resembled an overgrown square jeep with only a windshield to protect from whatever. Of course, it had big red crosses painted on the hood and on the sides. The back had a bench seat on each side, facing each other across a space that could hold a stretcher. My duty was to take the tagged guys from each morning's sick call to the nearby forward hospital. After that I was free to go anywhere with the truck and an unlimited trip ticket, which meant that I could get all the gas I wanted. My orders from the doctor, who was my CO, were to pick him up that evening at ten o'clock from his girlfriend's house in town. On many days, I set out to explore the countryside. At first, I would set out to visit one of the towns that I could see as a little nest of houses perched up in the nearby hills. But I discovered that after about two miles of ascent up the twisted roads, the engine would stop. I would have to let the truck roll backward, as there was no place to turn around on those narrow roads. I would often be going thirty to forty miles per hour backward for two or three miles before I could turn around and start the engine again. Once, on one of the uphill jaunts, I had some passengers who had imbibed some vino among themselves. They would offer me some of their libation with the advice that it would help me to really drive that "4 × 4." I would tell them that I didn't need that stuff and challenged them to suggest some maneuver that I could not do. I gained a reputation for driving the "fastest 'four' in the Second Battalion."

This is the way I looked in the summer of 1944.

I became friends of the family of my captain's girlfriend and I spent some pleasant evenings visiting with them. The front door of the house was a typical front door from the street, but upon entering, one was in the stable with three or four cows. The walkway through the stable was paved and the cows were not permitted to soil it. Then another door led into the living room. This arrangement allowed the use of the cow's body heat to help heat the home. I had many pleasant conversations with this man, his wife, and his seventeen-year-old daughter. My CO was courting the twenty-three-year-old daughter. In that part of Italy, custom prescribed very precise rules for courtship. Dating, as we know it, was not permitted. After two people persuaded their parents that they wanted to get seriously acquainted, they had to sign papers with the local priest, then the young man could visit the family and all of the exchange of pleasantries occurred in the girl's family circle. During the summer months, many families would dress up a bit and join the "promenade," a leisurely walk along the main streets of the town. The engaged couple could walk as part of the family procession.

My CO had signed courtship papers with a priest and was courting the older daughter. They were permitted to visit in another room and so had some privacy. After two or three weeks, my CO had an attack of conscience because he had a wife back in Harlem. So he told me to take the gifts that they had given him, to tell them the truth, and ask them to forgive him for lying to them. I told them the truth and delivered the mattress that they had given him to go on his canvas cot. (We all slept on cotton bags stuffed with straw, which became our body bags if we required burial.) That was the end of my visits with this family.

I had one more encounter with the family. I would sometimes put on my aid kit, go to town, and in the town square tell people that I was a doctor. I would put bandages on cuts and pack an aching tooth with powdered aspirin. But mostly I would commiserate with the local citizens. One afternoon the man of the house came to me and said that his older daughter was sick. I went to see her and she was sick; her temperature was 102°. I told him that I had to get the real doctor because I was not a doctor but I told him to give her fresh squeezed grape juice to drink until I could get the doctor. The father said, "OH NO, MORTE, MORTE." In other words, fresh squeezed grape juice would kill her.

But I knew that he had a wine press that used a big screw to press the grapes and not the bare feet that most winepresses used. I have watched barefooted men or women walking on the dusty roads, kicking horse dobs out of the way, and then climbing into the winepress to tramp the juice out of the grapes. From that time forward we called vino "toe juice"; we had seen the grape harvest and the winepresses. That is why the father said "Morte!" But I assured him that his juice was better since bare feet had not trodden his grapes.

When I got back to camp, my CO was on a three-day pass to Rome. Two days later, I persuaded him to go back, face the family, and treat the daughter. When the doctor got back and examined her, he found she had suffered from a blood clot during her menstrual period. Being a virgin, she needed medical attention. The doctor later told me that the grape juice had kept her alive for the three days before he could treat her. Se we healed the rift in our relationship with the family but our social visits did not continue.

On another posting, I was with the air base security unit at a different B-17 bomber field. Even though I had promised my mother (by mail) that I would not fly anymore, I could not resist the temptation and so I made three or four more flights on B-17s noncombat flights. I got to experience the different stations in the plane, such as sitting in the Plexiglas nose and firing the machine guns under the nose with tracer rounds into a puff of a cloud two or three hundred yards in front of us. Later I actually flew the plane for about fifty miles. On another trip I persuaded a buddy to go with me, his first time in a plane.

Remember that these planes had no upholstery or paneling so that the noise of the four engines was very loud and made conversation impossible. The nine-member crew used an intercom system with headphones and microphones for crewmembers. On most of my rides, there was no headphone available so it was on this day that my buddy put his mouth next to my ear and shouted as loudly as he could, "My ears hurt!." I did likewise and shouted, "What did you say?" He repeated his first sentence, which I then understood, so I said "swallow!" His reply, "What did you say?" "Swallow!" "What did you say?" I was chewing a stick of gum so the next time he opened his mouth I took the gum out of my mouth and stuck it in his mouth. Then, in a moment, relief showed on his face and a smile appeared.

We were both standing, looking out of the waist gunner's window, looking at the things we were flying over, when a P-51 flew a parallel course with us, and we could see that the pilot was black. That was the first time either of us had seen a black face in an airplane. The pilot had a blue silk scarf around his neck, and his wheels were down because he was about to land. He waved to us and then tipped his wing and disappeared toward the ground. It was the first time he had seen black faces in a B-17. We later realized that we were very near the P-51 strip of the 332nd fighter group, the Tuskegee Airmen's landing strip.

A detachment of out regiment guarded the 332nd base. I went twice on a truck with some of the guys who wanted to visit their buddies at the strip and I had the privilege of seeing some of the takeoffs and landings of the TA (Tuskegee Airmen) pilots. Once I was standing near a white P-51 pilot from a neighboring base, as we watched a flight of TA planes (four planes) who were returning from a mission. I later heard that they had flown the assigned bomber escort mission and having some gas left, decided to "go downstairs" to see what? (Bombing escort was done at twenty-nine thousand to thirty thousand feet) When they descended, they saw a German train chugging along so they strafed the engine. They could see steam jets shooting out of the bullet holes in several different directions and then the engine derailed. So when they came back to base they celebrated by buzzing the strip in flight formation. Then they came down and landed in the same formation. All four planes approached the end of the runway in formation but only two had their wheels down, so those two landed in formation together. The white pilot near me was looking with his eyes agog his mouth hanging open. The other two planes circled and landed in the same formation.

The men on guard duty worked a three-day shift. They would be on duty for forty-eight hours and off for twenty-four hours. While on duty, they would walk their post for two hours and be off for four. This continued around the clock so that every twenty-four hours they were on eight and off sixteen.

As a medic, I was free almost every day after morning sick call. A few times, I had to be on duty at a "pro" station for prophylactic treatment that was supposed to kill any germs resulting from a soldier's seventh commandment violations. Most soldiers totally ignored the "pro" stations and the only customer I had was a Senegalese soldier who couldn't speak English or Italian and who thought the "pro" station was a house of prostitution. He underwent the treatment and then began to mutter while standing there with his privates hanging out waiting for a lady to appear. I abandoned the premises and went next door to the MP station until he recovered from his disappointment. I admired those black troops from North Africa. They were tall and robust and could not understand the Jim Crowism that the army tried to instill into the Italian population. Certain towns became white friendly and other towns became black friendly. The Senegalese would go to a bar in any town and if it were the wrong town, a fight would erupt. Often two Senegalese would clear a bar of white troops. I heard of one who would take a white soldier by his ankles and use him like a two-handed club to clear the "enemy" from in front of him. So I did not want to take any chances with that brother in the pro station.

So the summer of 1944 was for me like being in a resort area. Sunny Italy lived up to its reputation because I remember an early shower in late April, soon after our arrival. My tent and blankets were floating. I had to wring them out and sleep wet that night. The latter rains did not come until sometime in September. During the summer, I flew over much of Bast Italia (lower Italy). I got to look into the cone of Mt. Vesuvius and look at Pompeii from two thousand feet. I visited, on the ground, a town called Cerignolia, site of a fort that was built about 1100 AD. The brick walls had narrow slits for firing ports because at that time bows and arrows were the weapons of choice.

I wasn't doing very much Sabbath keeping because there was no church to attend. Sometimes I could walk away from camp and spend some time alone. But one Sabbath morning I was just hanging around and watched as a story unfolded. A hand grenade is a pineapple-shaped metal container, filled with gunpowder, which fits snugly in a man's hand. It has a lever on the side, which will ignite a four-second fuse when lifted. The lever is lifted by a spring and held in place by a pin. When the hand grenade is used in combat, one has to pull the pin that will release the lever unless one holds it in place with his hand. The object is to pull the pin then throw the grenade. When the grenade leaves one's hand, the lever is released and the fuse will ignite and make a hissing sound for four seconds, then the grenade will explode and send metal fragments in all directions, usually mortally wounding anyone within four or five feet. We learned to unscrew the top of the grenade without pulling the pin and then we could dump the gunpowder out and play with it. I have made a trail on the ground with gunpowder. One could light one end of the trail with a match and it would burn with a low sparkly flame to the other end of the trail. If you tapped the flame with your foot, a small explosion would occur with a small pop. One time I tapped a part of a burning trail that was a little thicker and my foot received quite a jolt.

On this Sabbath morning, a certain captain was in his tent. The sides of the tent were rolled up so that one could see through the tent. He was drying himself with a towel, having just come from a shower. Somebody threw a hand grenade so that it rolled almost to his feet. It was hissing. He dropped his towel, fell to his knees, and tried to go under his canvas bunk so the bunk was tipped up on his back and his bare behind was plainly visible out in the company street. He started praying aloud. The grenade hissing stopped, then his praying stopped, and there was utter silence for about a whole minute. Then he stood up and began to utter words of profanity and damnation so much that it seemed as though the air turned blue around him. I shudder today to think that I found that scene highly hilarious—and it was the Sabbath. Today that language makes me shudder.

Later, during the summer, I got a three-day pass and visited Rome about six weeks after it was liberated from the Nazis. I visited St. Peter's Square, but did not enter the cathedral. I would so much rather see my front steps back in Detroit!

I had such a longing for a taste of homemade ice cream, that I got the addresses of twenty-two shops that might sell ice cream like the soda fountains at home. I finally found one that offered me an ice cream cone.

Back in the southern Italy, I found a shop, bargained with the proprietor, and bought a mandolin. I had not yet honed my bargaining skills so I got the price down only from 3200 lire to 1800 lire. Two months later, I bought a second mandolin for 1200 lire (about $12).

One payday afternoon, most of us had received our money, US $70 with the $20 overseas bonus. Suddenly, a soldier, a, cousin to the heavyweight-boxing champion Joe Lewis, fired two shots with his M-1 rifle. I was at least one hundred yards away from him, but I heard the bullets zip past my ear almost before I heard the shots. If my head had been over two or three inches, I would have been buried in a mattress bag somewhere in southern Italy.

By mid-September, the nights became chilly. We made makeshift stoves with quart-sized juice cans for the chimney. Our fuel was gasoline. The gasoline burned with a smoky yellow flame. The smoke condensed as soot in the tin can chimney and would close it after about a week of nightly fires. This would cause an explosion that would destroy the chimney, making a cloud of soot, and blowing the fire out. The guys would reassemble the chimney, relight the fire, and resume. Once or twice, the tents would ignite and be semi destroyed. I went to an army junkyard nearby and found a thirty-gallon oil drum and a length of four-inch iron sewer pipe. I had the sewer pipe welded to the oil drum and set it up in our tent as a stove. When our stove got stuffed with soot, it would explode just like all the rest, but the explosion would blow a big puff of soot out of the chimney—and clean it! All we had to do was to relight the fire.

Sometime after D-day the government declared that black troops could be trusted in combat. In August, part of the Ninety-second Division had been shipped to Italy and they had begun to fight the Germans north of Rome. Our regiment was ordered to enter combat with them. Our colonel requested that we receive retraining for six weeks since we had been assigned to garrison duty for over three years. The army's policy was to retrain any combat unit that was given two weeks of R & R as a break from combat and then they got two weeks of retraining before they returned to the front. We were denied any retraining but were ordered to reassemble and enter combat as soon as possible. So we began reassembly in October 1944. Some of the units of the 366th were recalled from southern France.

Sometime in late October or early November, our colonel gave a speech to the whole reassembled regiment. He lamented the fact that ninety-two young Italian women had come to him bearing the signed documents that were the equivalent of engagement agreements, and who were now pregnant but unmarried. It was too late to permit anyone to go back to the town or villages to marry their beloved if that had been their intention in the first place.

I remember passing through a railroad yard on the northern outskirts of Rome in a third-class coach on a train headed north. A five-hundred-pound bomb was lying on its side. The top was opened like a watermelon, the metal curved back over the sides, while the bottom half was full of water. Most bombs showered the surrounding countryside with pieces and fragments when they exploded, but much of this one had remained intact.

By Thanksgiving, we were camped a few miles from Pisa with its famous Leaning Tower. Part of our medical section was marched to the tower and I got to walk up the stairs to the top tier. While up there, I met a white soldier, also named Smith, whom I had met at Emanuel Missionary College two years earlier.

Thanksgiving Day dawned with a cold drizzling rain. We were living in pup tents again. There is very little that is more miserable and depressing than to live in a pup tent in a cold rain. There is no room to get out of bed without getting out of the tent. When we heard

chow call for our Thanksgiving dinner of roast turkey, mashed potatoes, gravy, etc., we had to get in line with our mess kits, dressed in
raincoats and helmets. It always seemed as though the helmet was
designed to drip inside the raincoat collar. There was just enough
rain to gently dilute the gravy on our potatoes. We had to stand
in the rain to eat because we could not stand in our tents. Each of
us was surrounded by ten to fifteen Italian civilians, also standing in
the rain. They were holding small buckets, or plates and spoons or
bowls, watching us eat, and hoping that we would scrape our left-
overs into their containers. We could trace the journey of our forks
up and down from mess kits to mouths by watching the movement
of their eyes.

One mean-spirited soldier took his half-full mess kit and dunked
it under the coffee grounds and dirty water in an almost full gar-
bage can. A small, old man reached his utensil down into the grayish
looking swill, fished out the mashed potatoes and piece of turkey,
brushed off the coffee grounds and walked away with the sad remnants of that dinner. I gave the rest of my food to a young woman
who was in the circle near me, then went back into my tent.

We made our way by slow stages toward the front. Some nights
we traveled in truck convoys; sometimes we walked. There is a certain kind of mind-set that seems to come upon new troops that are
on their way to battle. The object is to get rid of all excess baggage.
The first things to go were our gas masks. Anyone who would follow
our route the next day would see gas masks adorning all the bushes
and other artifacts along the sides of the road. The next day when
we bivouacked, we discarded our mess kits; I just kept a spoon that I
carried in my shoe top. By this time, we had been on C rations that
came in cans. Thanksgiving was the last time we had a mess hall to
cook for us. Our rations would come in cans and so we needed only
a can opener and a spoon. All of the card players discarded the joker
from their card decks. On November 30, 1944, we arrived at a stag-
ing area in the city of Barga, just four miles and over two hundred
meters below our destination, the town of Sommocolonia, which
was just yards away from the Germans.

We assembled after dark and heard a speech by the commanding general of the Ninety-second Division. He told us that he didn't ask for us, he didn't want us; we had too many high-ranking officers, etc. Those were the words that ushered us into combat. Then we started walking and soon found ourselves going up a cobbled stone trail that was the equivalent of climbing a gently sloped staircase. It was December 1, 1944, my father's birthday. I thought a little about the danger I was facing, but as so many soldiers do, I thought that while my companions would be the ones to get wounded or killed, it would not happen to me. Then, the fact that we had not had any training for months began to tell. I had to struggle to keep up and I could feel muscles that had not been used for a while begin to complain. I had about thirty pounds in my pack. Sometime during our struggle upward, we heard a cannon shot, the first sound of enemy fire. The quickest way for me to follow the instructions that were Standard Operating Procedure (SOP) when under attack was to "assume the prone position," which we had dubbed "Hit the prone!", was for me to fall over backwards because that was quickest way for me to "Hit the prone."

The five-hundred-year-old road or trail, the only road to
Sommocolonia in *1944*

• • •

PART III – THE FRONT AND COMBAT

CHAPTER 7
Sommocolonia

We finally arrived in Sommocolonia, at the top of that climb late at night and weary. We, four of us, were the medics assigned to an infantry company that was to occupy and hold the town. It was a key position in the German defense line in Italy at that time. The Germans called it "the Gothic Line."

The Gothic Line stretched across the upper third of the Italian boot and was to be held at all costs. Any German officer who spoke of retreat was to be summarily shot. The strategy on the Allied side was to hold the Gothic Line until spring when tanks could maneuver again. The winter operation became a "holding front." Sommocolonia was an ancient town that normally had a population of about 250. The four-hundred- or five-hundred-year-old houses were made of stone. (There was one brick house in town.) The walls were twelve to eighteen inches thick.

The streets were narrow, three to six feet wide, cobblestone, and either ascending or descending. Some of the streets consisted in a series of wide steps. The only level place outside the houses was the town square.

This is one of the wider streets.

The only vehicle that could reach the town was a jeep and it could not go very far from the town square. In some places, the houses were built over the street so that one would walk through a tunnel for a short distance. All of our supplies and food came to us by mule back and the trail that we had climbed became known as the mule trail after the war when a new road for automobiles was built.

The four of us medics were billeted in a house on the rear side of town, away from the Germans. A Catholic priest and his house-keeper also lived there. This priest was the spiritual father of the town, and people regarded him almost as the mayor, chief of police, and leading official. He was the only visible authority for the town.

At that time, the Italian people were pro-Allies about 9–1. We did know it at the time, but there was one prominent citizen in the town that was pro-Fascist. I suspected that the priest was also a Fascist. The Italian citizens could more or less freely cross the Gothic Line and visit relatives or friends in the German-occupied sectors. On one or two occasions, the light switches in the house where we were billeted would click the dots and dashes of Morse code. I believe that the host of the house was sending to the Germans or Fascist.

Fireplaces heated the houses. The cook stoves were built into fire pits that burned small pieces of wood and had a grating or grill over them. Sometimes an open fire pit would be in the middle of a room with low wooden racks placed around it so that families could sit in a circle with their feet on the rack.

I went out one day in search of firewood. I was helping myself from a woodpile at a nearby house when a young woman came out and begged me not to take their firewood. I told her OK, but asked her to show me some wood that I could take. She led me to a neighbor's woodpile.

Our food was "10-in-1" rations. They came in a box that was enough food for one man for ten days or ten men for one day. It was much tastier than the C rations we had gotten tired of. We usually heated the food in their cans in hot water before we opened them. I saw a Bill Mauldin cartoon in the *Stars and Stripes* in which one soldier tells a buddy to be careful when he dropped a can of stew into the coffee because there was also a chicken stewing in the bottom!

It was during my days with the medical team stationed in the priest's house that I met Giovanni (not his real name). He was a sixteen-year-old partisan who had been fighting the Germans for more than two years. He showed me a crease in his chest caused by a beam that fell on his chest and broke all the ribs on one side. The same explosion had killed his father. One night while we were talking, something hit the front door. He opened the door and jumped out with his rifle at the ready. I remonstrated with him that he could have been shot before his feet landed in the street. He assured me

...lief that he had already been "killed" and that

...cedure upon hearing a sound or a knock was to the daily password—which would be the first word or a ...ke "captains courageous." The Germans sometimes got our password before we did. One night it would have backfired on them. The password was "Mohave Desert." Our guys pronounced it "Mojave Dessert" A German who answered desert, the correct password that night, would have gotten shot. When a knock or a sound was heard, one would say the first word and the person outside would say the second word.

We had boxes of blood serum in our forward aid station. One day we received orders to take the boxes of serum to the pack mules and send them down the hill. Two or three days later, we received boxes of serum to replace what we had sent. We noticed a big letter "C" marked on each box or container, indicating that we now had "colored" serum.

We have not said anything about contact with the enemy up to this point and one might get the impression that "holding" the front was without danger. That was not the case. The Germans were across a small valley and beyond the top of a higher hill that was just beyond the Sommocolonia Hill. Our ammunition was rationed. (Our general thought to save the army some money, albeit by putting at risk the lives of those colored soldiers in his command.) Every day at 11:55 a.m., we would fire up the hill at the Germans. All guns, from carbines to M-1 rifles, to 105 howitzers would fire their sixteen rounds at the enemy. Then we could swab out our guns, and go back to our daily activities, standing guard, cooking, eating, and playing cards. The medics had life easy. We took turns at staffing the aid station and had the rest of the time free. The Germans would return fire every day at 4:55 p.m. for five minutes the way we had in the morning. The country was so hilly that the Germans could not use any big guns like their infamous 88s to shell us. Instead, they used mortars. These would hit the sides of the stone houses and clean the ivy and lichen off the stone, but did very little other damage.

At night, each side would send out a patrol to sneak into enemy territory to try to spy out the land and, if possible, bring back a prisoner or two. An American combat patrol was twenty-six men. I never was tempted to go with a patrol. I was not praying during this time and I was not ready to risk my life. One day I was ordered to accompany a patrol planned for that night to bring back the body of a dead man who had been left in enemy territory for two days. I informed the lieutenant that I was not responsible for dead people. My duty was to treat the wounded. He really needed to call for Graves Registration personnel. He called his superior officer who told him that the private was right—so I never went on a patrol.

After about ten days, I was ordered to serve as the medic for a machine gun squad stationed on the side of town facing the Germans. There were nine men in the squad. Since I was an unarmed medic and did not have to stand guard duty, I volunteered as the cook and mess sergeant for the squad. We used the dishes left in the house by the former occupants. I would use the food from the 10-in-1 ration boxes and cook three meals a day we ate on china plates with forks and spoons. I did not relish the idea that a lucky hit by a German mortar shell could explode in the house and destroy clean dishes that I had washed so I would wash the dishes just before each chow time.

One of the last duties I performed before coming to the machine gun squad was to transport a wounded soldier. This 250-pound sergeant had become paranoid with fear and had shot himself in the foot with a British Sten gun. I was given three infantry men, and the four of us had to carry the heavy sergeant on a stretcher on the mule trail down the mountain, where he could be put in an ambulance. The three helpers cursed the sergeant so soundly during that cobblestone descent that I felt sorry for him. He was consigned to be a part of a structure that stops a river from flowing. His maternal ancestry was canonized repeatedly, and he was condemned as one who had committed incest many times. All this came while each of us was struggling down the hill with our corner of the 250-pound stretcher.

One of the sergeants in the machine gun squad was concerned with my being unarmed, because he believed I was in greater danger than they were. Many people, both civilian and military, had expressed the same idea that one is more vulnerable while unarmed. My answer to them is that every dead man that I saw had a weapon in his hands or one very near at hand. Even so, one of the sergeants gave me a .45 automatic pistol with its holster. I wore it for a few days but for some reason I felt very uncomfortable with it. Even though I was not praying, I felt that if God was going to keep me, He could do it better if I remained as a conscientious objector, unarmed. I finally told the sergeant that it was too heavy for me to carry with my aid kits.

I was walking through the town one afternoon and decided to visit the ancient tower that was the tallest building on the German side of the town. It had been built around the year 1100. It was a square tower and I climbed to the second floor, which was a large room with an opening like a picture window that overlooked the valley between us and the enemy hill. A forward observer was there who had just received orders from his headquarters to direct artillery fire on a two-story house that was in the middle of the valley. I watched as he telephoned the guns a mile or more to our rear. He gave some coordinates and then rapped out, "Fire one for effect!"

The first shell landed about seventy yards beyond the house. After he made some corrections in the coordinates, the next shot was only six or eight yards in front of the house. The next shot was dead on the house. He ordered several more shots to hit the house until the roof and most of the second floor were destroyed, and the house was burning. Only parts of the first-floor walls were left standing after the fire burned for a while. This tower room later became John Fox's death chamber.

• • •

PART IV – CAPTURE AND PRISONER OF WAR

CHAPTER 8
Fateful Christmas and Capture

Our commanders ordered us to mount an offensive on Christmas Eve. In the few days before Christmas, we made preparations. We got troop reinforcements. We received some extra medical supplies. The machine gunners twisted their gun belts to be sure that no round would get stuck in the webbing and cause the gun to jam.

I began to contemplate having to advance up that hill under enemy fire. The thought crossed my mind that I wasn't really ready to meet my Savior face-to-face. I would put off such thoughts with the soldier's usual comforting thought that each one of my buddies would get hit, but somehow, I would not get hurt at all. So I would dismiss the thought that I should repent of my sins and put myself in God's care.

Late in the afternoon of December 23, the attack was officially cancelled and things returned to normal by Christmas Eve. After dark on Christmas Eve, I visited a house where two young women resided, sixteen and eighteen years of age. One or two of their friends who were partisans were also present. I was the only buffalo. (members of the ninety-second infantry division wore a black buffalo shoulder patches and were known as black buffalos) I had my mandolin and we played and sang Christmas carols for a couple of hours before I went back to my station and my sleeping bag. Christmas Day dawned, and the Germans celebrated by shelling us with mortar shells intermittently throughout the day. Our Christmas dinner of turkey, mashed potatoes and gravy, etc. could not reach our hill until after dark because of the shelling. At dinnertime that evening, I served our usual evening fare and promised the guys that we would have Christmas dinner for breakfast the next morning.

Early the next morning, December 26, 1944, I got up while it was still dark to get a pail of water. I needed to wash enough dishes for breakfast, our belated Christmas Day breakfast. Motor shells were still falling intermittingly, so I put my helmet on, took the empty bucket and started out to walk the few hundred yards to the town spigot through the narrow twisted cobblestone streets, between the closed-up and silent houses.

One of the two spigots for the whole town.

On the way, a motor shell struck the upper-story wall of a house almost over my head. Some of the pieces fell near my feet. I picked up a ragged piece of metal, then dropped it because it was hot. I filled the bucket and walked back to the house. I hung the bucket over the fireplace. If one were to stand facing the window, the fireplace was to the left. The window had wooden shutters on the outside and had a raincoat nailed across the frame on the inside. The room was about 12 × 12 feet. A door to the right rear led to a ten-to twelve-foot hallway, which ended at the door to the street.

The mortar shelling had become much more frequent by this time. There were three of us in the room that passed for a kitchen, as there was a dry sink under the window. We had all put our helmets on because of the increased shelling. Some inner voice prompted me to put my aid kit on and so I said to the sergeant, "I am going to put my aid kit on because somebody is going to get hurt with all of this stuff."

I walked over to the wall opposite the window, bent down, and leaned over with my right hand to pick up the aid kit canvas harness. Just at that moment, a 120 mm German mortar shell hit the window and exploded.

I saw a flash of fire and heard a deafening sound. It seemed as though a strong force shoved me against the wall. I heard metal hit my helmet. The sergeant was standing in front of the window slightly to one side. Another private was standing near the fireplace warming his hands. He received a cut on the back of his head. The sergeant received several holes in his chest. He had been drinking water from a dipper and the little finger of his right hand was hanging by just a piece of skin. He had a hole in the upper thigh of his leg that was big enough to enclose a 4 × 4 bandage. I got hit on my right cheek, my right elbow, and my right upper leg just below the hipbone. I had a small cut on my left buttock, a piece of glass was embedded underneath my right eye, and my right ear lobe was cut.

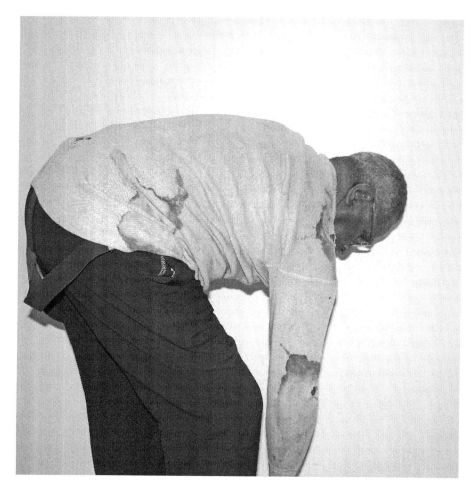

The sergeant hollered, "I'm hit!"

I did too. When I stood up, I could see an enlarged opening where the window had been. Daybreak was just beginning and I could see Germans on the hill in front of us. I could feel blood running down both legs and my right arm. My right hand was completely numb. (I had been hit on the crazy bone of my elbow). I put my left hand up to my cheek and it seemed as though my finger went into my mouth through the hole in my right cheek. About this time, we heard feet running in the street past our door. Then we heard gunfire down the street in front of our house. We could hear two men talking as they fired. They were speaking German. The rest of the squad had come into the room and the tech sergeant said, "I better ask these partisans what's going on!"

I told the sarge that those voices were speaking German—not Italian. Men were screaming and dying. Bullets were ricocheting as I was dressing the sergeant's wounds. I had to tie bandages with my left hand and my teeth. In the midst of this battle, while all this was happening, I began to realize that I was dying. My pulse was becoming weaker as I was losing blood and finally I couldn't detect it anymore. I was the medic and there was no one else present to dress my wounds. A terrible dread came over me as I realized that I was about to die and then face Jesus. He would have a frown on His face, which meant eternal damnation for me. I tried to pray, but kept remembering all of the wrong things that I had done, and all of the times I had refused and neglected to pray.

Then my thoughts would be interrupted by the terrible battle that was raging through that part of town. The Germans had set up a machine gun right outside the street door and were firing down the street toward the town square. Then they advanced the machine gun and I heard a telephone in operation. A little while after I had bound up the sergeant's wounds, the rest of the squad made us as comfortable as they could and told us that they were going to try to escape out the back way. So the three of us were left and the others departed. I don't know to this day if any of them made it out of town.

It is hard to explain the terror and the struggle that was going on in my mind, knowing that I would face eternal destruction in a few minutes. I tried to pray, to ask God to hear me, even though I had spurned His pleadings for me to repent and accept His loving care for me before the dangers of combat. Yet God answered those prayers.

Years later, I realized that God led me to bend over to pick up my aid kit at just that precise moment, putting me in the position that let me survive the blast.

The reason I didn't bleed to death afterward, was because my father and mother were praying for me at home. The intercessory prayers of my parents saved my life.

God's direct intervention also kept me from bleeding to death after the explosion. The piece of metal that entered my back traveled about five inches through my flesh before it stopped. I bear the scars to this day, the entry scar, the incision scar where it was removed, and the piece of metal itself. If I had been standing, that piece of metal from the explosion would have killed me. It would have penetrated my heart.

This piece of metal stayed in my back for ten years. It is pictured with a purple heart, a bronze star, and the POW medal along with a stalag tag, all of which I received much later.

After the rest of our squad left the house, the Germans continued to advance past the door. I expected to lose consciousness from loss of blood, and I pleaded with God to forgive me for neglecting to hear Him and for ignoring Him—to please forgive me and accept my repentance. Simultaneously I had great fear of being discovered by the Germans and summarily shot.

Then, I finally realized that God still loved me. He accepted me. He forgave my sin. And I was ready to die in peace. A great calmness came over me. I knew that I was going to die, but I was not afraid of death anymore. I knew that in the second that I lost consciousness, Jesus would awaken me, and that He would have a smile on His face. I prayed that my death wouldn't hurt. We were all hoping that our troops would rally and drive the Germans back. We had been told that the Germans did not take black prisoners. We didn't know whether this was white folks' propaganda to make us fight or the truth. The sounds of the battle were receding as the Germans occupied more of the town. Every once in a while a German would kick or hit the front door and holler something, but they did not try to enter the house. The three of us moved across the hall to a room with a window wall facing the street.

My wounds got no dressing because there was no one to dress them. We had plenty of blankets so we made ourselves as comfortable as possible on the floor. The hole in my upper thigh had a few pieces of metal and the torn edges of my pants and under garments dried and caked in the blood. Every time I moved or turned over, the torn muscles in that dried blood hole would hurt. I would grit my teeth because of the pain. Every time I gritted my teeth, the cut on my ear would open and several more drops of blood would flow from my ear, depending on the position of my head. Those few drops would dry and stop the bleeding. By the next morning, my face resembled a burnt down candle. The coagulated blood had spread over the right side of my face and filled my right eye socket so that I couldn't open my eye. I had to left-handedly dig my eye open.

The other two wounded men with me looked like they were forty years old because of the fear and dread they felt. We had debated what we should do if the Germans entered the house. At first the "majority" decided that we must die fighting. I pointed out the facts. Our rifles needed cleaning because of the plaster dust from the wall cracked by the explosions. Two of us who were right handed could not use our right hands. Our only means of defense meant that we would have to throw hand grenades through a doorway with our left hands. I pointed out to them that we were in danger of missing the door opening and having the grenades kill us instead of the enemy. I finally persuaded them to agree that we would surrender. We knew that we were going to die. The objective was to die with the least amount of pain. I predicted that the Germans would put us against the wall that was across the five-foot-wide street and shoot us in the back. That way we would hardly feel any pain. I knew in my heart that a split second after the bullet entered my heart that I would awake in Glory. (Remember that the time that we are in a grave lasts but a moment.) We had made this decision during the afternoon of December 26, 1944.

By 10:30 that morning, the battle seemed to be in the distance. Finally, our artillery got their ammunition and began to fire into the town. (We had called for fire on the hillside in front of us before daylight that morning because the Germans had been advancing down that hill under cover of darkness and had set off trip flares that told they were there.) I remember going upstairs and, while looking out across the rooftops toward our rear, seeing an artillery shell coming toward me. It hit a chimney about two hundred yards away. I went downstairs. A moment after I got back to the room, a shell hit the upstairs and shook the house. Cracks appeared in the plaster on the walls and ceiling. I reached over, took the sergeant's hand, and said, "This is it!"

The next shell landed in the street in front. The huge oaken wardrobe that was blocking the front window moved several inches into the room. No more shells came near us that day. Two or three shells landed in other parts of the town and then the firing stopped for about fifteen minutes.

We then heard a salvo of shells that landed four or five hundred yards to our left flank. They were concentrated on the observation tower. Then the guns went silent and they were not fired again during the battle. I didn't learn until fifty years later that the salvo of shells had killed John Fox, the forward observer in the tower that morning—he had ordered the fire on his own position. That salvo had killed him and more than forty-six Germans.

The tower after more than fifty years.

His widow, Arlene Fox, received a belated Congressional Medal of Honor for him fifty years after the war.

The Germans continued to advance past our house. By late afternoon, we heard only sporadic and distant small arms fire. The traffic continued outside our door but we were not disturbed. The next morning, after I had dug my eye open, we drank some canned pineapple juice and settled down to wait—and to hope for a German retreat. Maybe, about eight or nine o'clock (During the whole ordeal I had no watch. I had lent it to one of the guys who stood guard on Christmas night. He had forgotten to return it during the trauma and turmoil of the battle the next morning.)

Two German soldiers opened the front door and began advancing slowly down the hall toward the door to our room. The time had come. We were about to be killed. When they got almost to our door, I hollered "kamarad." They ran from the building. Very soon, they returned with reinforcements, and shouted something in German. I shouted the question, "Parlo Italiano?" One voice answered "Ci!" So we conversed in Italian. He asked "How many are you?" I replied that there were three. He next ordered us to come out with our hands up. I told him that one couldn't walk. By this time, the sergeant's leg had gotten as stiff as a board. But we were told to come out anyway. I had not been able to put my shoes on that morning because my feet had swollen. And so we, dragging the sergeant between us, got to the front door. I stood in my stocking feet. When the three of us got to the open front door at the end of the hall, we looked into the barrels of five different guns in the hands of five German soldiers. I expected to be dead in less than one minute and was not afraid. I thought that in the next split second after I lost consciousness, Jesus would be waking me up. I tried to smile and found that half of my face could not bend because of the caked blood. One of the committee of five who welcomed us at the door was a corporal who could speak Italian. He told us to take the sergeant back, and then the two of us should come out with our hands up. I thought they would have us face the stone wall, which was behind them on the other side of the narrow cobblestone street, so that they could shoot us in the back.

Instead, they told us to walk in front of them, with our hands up. I had some thick wool socks on my feet and about one-eighth of an inch of snow had fallen during the night. As we walked, we had to step over the bodies of two or three buffalos who had died in the fighting the day before. I remember stepping into the dried blood that surrounded each body that we stepped over. My back seemed to feel a tingle that traveled up and down my spine as my back anticipated where the bullets would crash through.

We had to walk the equivalent of three or four city blocks until we came to the town square. The town square was a level square with buildings on four sides, and at that time there was a statue of some kind in the center of the square. We could see openings to three or four streets. When we entered, there were dead bodies lying where they had fallen the day before. On one side were two dead Germans, one lying across the other and a German soldier was digging a grave in which to bury them. Four or five buffalos lay in the dried blood pools where they had fallen. At least two partisans' bodies lay where they had fallen. They included Giovanni, the teen who believed he couldn't be killed.

Giovanni's body had fallen to his knees and then bent forward until his head was resting on the pavement. Just then, a German soldier came up to him, grabbed him by his hair, and jerked his head up. I could see the hole in his forehead that had killed him. That was when I recognized who he was. He had an American hand grenade in his hand. The German took the hand grenade and stuck it in his belt. Then he jerked Giovanni's head backward until his body was laying face upward and the back of his head was resting on the pavement.

We were directed to the other side of the square where we were searched and then permitted to put our hands down. We were on the steps of a small porch-like landing where we sat for the next two hours or so. The corporal struck up a conversation with me. He told me that we were to become prisoners of war and that we would be transported to a prison camp; while there, we would be able to write home.

He asked me why I was over there fighting in the war. I told him about America's duty to liberate England and France from German domination.

Then he asked, "Why are you really over here?"

I told him because I was drafted and got sent there by the army. He said that he was fighting for the same reason. He was twenty-two and had been in the army for five years. He had seen combat on the Russian front. He then asked me to give him my fountain pen. I asked him what could I write with—as a prisoner of war, how would I be able to write home? He let me keep the pen. Later, a German soldier just walked up to me and took my pen. I asked the corporal more than once about the wounded sergeant we had left. He assured me that he would be transported to a POW hospital.

During the time the two of us were sitting on the steps, German soldiers were coming and going through the square. One dead buffalo was lying about two feet from the corner of the step I was sitting on. Later the corporal offered each of us a slab of bread (a thick slice). I took a bite of my bread and then I held it out toward the dead man and with "gallows humor" told him to "Have a bite."

My buddy next to me hit me and said it was sacrilegious to joke with the dead. I told him I would be disturbed only if he had answered me!

After a while—about the third or fourth time I asked about the sergeant—the corporal got permission to escort us back to the house. When we got back, we cheered the sarge as best we could. I was able to put my shoes on and I stuffed all of my pockets with whatever eatables I could carry—hardtack, crackers, hard candy—I put two envelopes of sulfa powder in my inner shirt pocket and forgot that they were there until about three weeks later when I really needed them.

We made the sergeant as comfortable as possible and told him what we had been told about his being transported to a POW hospital. The next day, when I passed the house for the last time, I saw it had suffered a direct hit from a five-hundred-pound bomb and was mostly rubble. I realized months later when I got home and called his mother that he had died in that house. She had received no word except that he was missing in action. I knew that he had not appeared in the hospital chain for POWs that I had gone through, so I told her that he was dead and gave her some of the details of his final moments on this earth. He was her only son, and she was a widow.

We walked back to the square. A short time later, the corporal and I, accompanied by a small squad of German soldiers, were sent on a mission to find buffaloes that were still holed up in parts of the town. I was told to shout that if they surrendered they would be made prisoners and not killed. I shouted, "They say that you will be made prisoners of war and not shot." We were walking just out of the town square when I heard a plane flying over. I looked up and said in my mind P-47. When I looked down again, every German had disappeared. Then someone snatched me into a basement stairway. I realized that the United States Air Force was now my enemy.

We walked around the outside of the town pausing frequently for me to act as the town crier, to ask other soldiers to surrender. We came to a house that had a shuttered upstairs window facing us. There was some conversation in German, then the German lieutenant who was standing near me took his machine pistol and cut a round hole in the shutter by spacing the bullets about two inches apart. Then the round piece fell into the opening.

We wound around the northern perimeter of the town and then turned in toward the interior again. The soldiers began to enter some houses and look for food or other loot. Two men came out of the basement of one house with a five-gallon bottle of wine. The bottle had a basket woven around it because otherwise there was no way to carry it. For a while, I was left with just one soldier to guard me. I asked him for some water. Due to my loss of blood, I had become intensely thirsty. I asked two or three times for some water. He finally took off his canteen cup, which held more than a pint, filled it with the liberated wine and gave it to me. I thought that this would make me as high as a kite but I needed the water, so I drank it. I did not get any effect of the alcohol at all. I believe that God nullified the alcohol for my body.

Soon after this, I was taken to a house just off of the square. It was built so that one entered the first floor from the street but there was a basement that could be entered from the rear of the house at ground level because of the slope of the land. The Germans had captured another buffalo and had two of them in the basement. They stopped me on the first floor to have my wounds dressed by a German medic for the first time.

I took my field jacket off and my shirt and undershirt so that he could bandage my shoulder. Then I put those things back on and started taking off my pants and underwear. This was very painful because the ragged edges of the holes in the various layers of my clothing, as well as two or three piece of metal, were caked into the dried blood. I was trying to gently and slowly remove the pieces and cloth ends. The medic gently but firmly helped me. Just then, a P-47 roared overhead just above the rooftops. The medic stopped what he was doing and bolted for the stairway to the basement and motioned for me to follow him. So the wound just below my hip did not get cleansed of the material caked in it. I slowly put my clothes back together and made my way down the stairs to the basement. I was directed to lie on the floor in the middle of the room.

The other two buffalos were already there and there were ten or twelve German troops lying on the floor. On one side of the room toward the back wall was a wooden oak door. The planks of the door were about two inches thick. Soon another German came running down the steps and ran across the room to the opposite wall to assume the prone position. On the way, he stepped in the middle of my back. Then we heard the roar of another plane, and after about twenty seconds, a terrible explosion.

A five-hundred-pound bomb had hit the house next door. We could see it because the oaken door had shattered and disappeared in a cloud of splinter and dust. We could look out of the doorway and see the remnants of the stone walls of what had been a bungalow. The base of the walls were two to four feet high. The rest of the house was rubble. The P-47 single-engine fighter planes that carried out the bombing missions were armed with eight .50-caliber machine guns. Each plane carried a five-hundred-pound bomb fastened underneath. Our town was so situated that a plane could fly at high speed in the valley then swoop up and over the town. Sometimes the first hint of an attack by a plane was the splatter of the .50-caliber bullets striking the houses and the streets. Then one would hear the roar of the plane engine as it zoomed a hundred or so feet overhead. Then, about twenty to thirty seconds later, the bomb would explode.

Later that day we were moved to another part of town where we were placed in a room on the second floor of a house that was also used as their headquarters.

Our room was at one corner of the house and their HQ was at the opposite corner, so that our two rooms were next to each other only at the one corner.

The repaired bomb blast that killed a German officer and
wounded others.

By this time, they had captured two or three more buffalos. There were two or three more bombing missions that day. The next day, December 28, I learned that a plane could announce its presence by the rattling and ricocheting of the bullets in the streets. This time the bomb made a direct hit on our building on the room that was the enemy HQ. A German officer was killed and an enlisted man was wounded.

I was lying on the floor in the middle of the room, and the blast threw me against one wall. The walls of the building were made of stone, about eighteen inches thick. In one part of the wall, an indentation was built in to fashion a place for shelving. There were knickknacks on the shelves. The shelves were about twelve inches wide at the back and about eighteen inches wide at the front. The wall behind the shelves was only four inches thick. When the bomb exploded, the wall behind the shelves disappeared and the knickknacks were still in place even though they were covered with dust.

Later that day three or four more men were captured. By dusk, there were ten of us. We were walked by the guards to a position near the square and there we sat or lay on the street and some rubble of a bombed-out house. My corporal interpreter came and handed me a Red Cross flag. He said that they had decided to retreat from the town and leave us there. The flag was to signal to whatever Allied soldiers came to reoccupy the town; they would see the flag and not shoot us. I didn't dare believe that our ordeal was over but I relayed the news to the others. About an hour after dark, a German soldier came and, without a word, took the flag.

• • •

CHAPTER 9
Five More Steps – Then Death!

A short while later my corporal came and asked me if I thought I could walk seven kilometers. I told him I thought so.

A short time later, we were told to start walking. There were three platoons of German soldiers. We were in the middle of the middle platoon. As we passed through the square for the last time, I remember seeing some rubble that partially covered a jeep in the middle of the square. I watched a German soldier move a big paving stone, place a land mine in its spot, and then carefully put the stone back on top of the mine. On the way out of town, we passed the remains of the house where I had left the sergeant. It had received a direct hit from a bomb and it was almost flattened. I hoped they had taken the sergeant out before the bomb hit. I learned, six months later that his body was in that rubble.

As we passed by, I silently said good-bye to my Bible, my mandolin, and to a fruitcake that an aunt had sent me from California. Just at the edge of town, we were lined up, single file, and each man received two cases that contained three 120 mm mortar shells (each like the shell that had hit me.) I got one case. Then we started walking, single file, up and down the winding footpath through the mountains. I immediately began to struggle to keep up. I was at the end of the prisoner line and my German corporal was right behind me. He was armed with an American carbine that he had captured and he gently prodded me with it. He would also tell me to hurry. And so we began the journey that turned out to be the worst night that I have spent on this earth.

At the beginning, we would frequently stop to rest in our climb. At the first stop, they issued orders to relieve each prisoner of one of the mortar shell cases, which made each man's load about forty pounds lighter. Then they made me keep my one load until the second or third halt. To relieve us, they would open each case and toss the mortar shells down into the valley. The shells were disassembled from their tail fins. My thirst became intense. We halted once to rest about eight to ten feet from a small waterfall, but we could not leave the path to get any water. A little distance farther, we passed a horse-watering trough that appeared to be lined with green moss. I dipped up some water with my helmet and drank it. Awhile later, I saw that we were walking through a muddy puddle in the trail. I scooped up some of that and drank it.

After two to four hours on the single-file trail, we came to a road. We stopped for another rest and I went to sleep. A short time later, probably about ten minutes, we were awakened and put in formation on the road. We were in two columns, as were the Germans, still in the middle of the middle platoon. The lieutenant gave the order "Marche!"

We started walking down the road. In the American Army, when on a route march, we walked fifty minutes and rested ten minutes every hour. The German Army walked until they reached their destination.

At first, one of the other buffalos would support me by walking beside me while I half leaned on his shoulder. They would switch every ten minutes or so. The lieutenant who set the pace at the head of the column came back and told my corporal who was right behind me that if I could not support myself he was to shoot me and leave me beside the road.

I then began to concentrate on trying to keep up. I could feel nothing from my waist down. It seemed as though I was using wooden legs. I started out by looking ahead to the second telephone pole. I would concentrate on reaching that second pole. Then I would decide whether I was just too tired to go on and to let them shoot me so that I could wake up in heaven. Or I would choose to struggle for two more poles. After about six or eight poles I realized I could not last for two poles. My mind told me that I didn't have enough strength to cover the distance of two more telephone poles. So I concentrated on getting to the next pole.

After the third or fourth pole, I realized that I was just too tired and weak to go the distance to the next telephone pole, so I determined to go fifteen steps and then to decide whether I would live or die. So I counted fifteen steps. Then fifteen more steps. Then fifteen more steps. After awhile, I reasoned, I am too tired to go fifteen steps. I will just go ten steps and then decide to live or to die. After a bit, I realized that I could not do ten steps. Every time I would slow down just a little, the corporal's carbine would nudge my back. In a little while, I knew that I was too tired to go ten steps so I determined I would concentrate on making five steps and then decide to live or die. So I put all of my energy and concentration and determination into counting five steps, then I would decide to do just five more steps. Then five more steps, then five more steps, then five more steps, for the rest of that night. Sometime in the early morning, well before daybreak, I began to realize that I could not continue much longer. I began to reason that five more steps was too much. I was running out of energy and the will to continue. I happened to put my hand into one of my side jacket pockets and touched a cellophane-wrapped piece of hard candy. (God's direct presence in my life) I put it in my mouth and it seemed as though energy and strength flowed from my mouth down my throat and all over my body.

Then I was able to continue to make a life-or-death decision every five steps. I could not think of a future or wonder what else was in my pocket or when this journey would end. I had to concentrate on making five steps in keeping up with the German route step pace of about four miles per hour. I did not have any mental energy to pray. All of my conscious thought was "one two three four five." Somehow, by deciding to count five more steps or, in other words, deciding to live five more steps every fifth step, I managed to stay in the formation and reach a town well after sunup.

During the night, I didn't pray. I concentrated on walking. I knew that God put that candy in my hand when it was needed most because my body was about to completely run out of energy. I know that God was with me every step I took, and I should have learned then what it means to pray without ceasing. My sole concentration was on counting five steps and then five more steps.

Each time I could think only that if I struggled to make five more steps, then I could rest by letting them shoot me.

Finally, the sun did come up and I continued to count five steps. After a while we came to a town and houses appeared on the sides of the road that had become a street. We finally were directed to enter a room on the ground floor of a house that held nine other buffalos and practically no furniture. I saw a dirty quilt from a baby's crib that somebody had used for a mat to repair their car because it was filthy dirty with oil stains and grease spots. I spread it on the concrete floor, and put my head on it and was fast asleep in short order.

· · ·

CHAPTER 10
The Journey Continues

After a little while, we were awakened and ordered out in the street to march to the other side of town. One of the other nine buffalos didn't have a field jacket or overcoat—in other words he was in his shirtsleeves. I had put my blanket over my shoulders, but when I saw him, I gave it to him to put over his shoulders. He kept it and used it for many days.

As we were walking through the streets, the women of the town were lined up on the sides of the street in one section. It was probably near the town water source. The Germans had told them that we were the enemy who had bombed their town and caused their misery. So they began to spit in our faces and hiss at us. Soon all the men's faces but mine were dripping with saliva. Three or four times a woman would approach me with her mouth full of spit but when she looked at my blood-covered face, she drew back in horror. Nobody spat in my face.

We walked to the other end of the town, into an old castle, and they herded us into a room inside a round tower that was a part of the castle. The room was about twenty feet in diameter. It was unheated but we were sheltered from the wind and could find some comfort sitting or lying on the floor. We had not had access to food or water since leaving Sommacolonia the night before.

Some time in the late afternoon, I began to distribute the food that I had stuffed in my pockets two days before. This was December 29, 1944. I was able to give all nineteen in our group at least a half of a hardtack or one piece of candy, etc. A little later four Italian men were put in the room with us. They had on blue coveralls. They were not soldiers. They were mostly silent and hardly spoke to each other or to us. I surmised after they had spent about ten days with us that they were from some kind of mental institution.

We spent the night in the tower and after noon of the next day, they gave us some bread. After dark, we were formed up in the street, marched eight or ten miles, and then we were herded into a building. After daybreak, we realized it was a stable. It had straw on the floor mixed with dried horse dobs and several coconut-sized rocks. This was our home for four or more days.

Here I had the second clean bandage applied to the hole in my shoulder. A bandage was also applied over the hole in my upper thigh.

After a day or so, I picked up one of the round stones and found that it was much lighter than a stone. I banged it against an edge and broke it open. It was a round loaf of bread. I broke off some of the inside and began to eat it. It was so dry that I would hold a piece under the spigot located just outside the door and run water over it. Then I could bite and eat it like some very firm bread. The other guys asked me how I could eat that "manure" (not the term they used), but after a while, they joined in eating some. The Germans were feeding us irregularly, usually once a day.

It was here in the stable where we received our first interrogation. Three soldiers, different from our guards, came to perform the interrogation. We had been put in custody of home guards when we arrived in the first town at the end of the nightlong march. I didn't get to say good-bye to my corporal. One of the questioners had a great big book, like an old-fashioned bank ledger, which he opened. The soldier who was asking the questions spoke English with a slight accent. We found out later that he had lived in Chicago for about seven years.

According to the Geneva Convention, a prisoner is required to give only his name, rank, and serial number. We were asked who our company commander was, where we got our basic training, and many other questions. One buffalo, when asked who his company commander was, replied, "Tim Tyler." The interrogator said, "You lie. He is a character in the funny papers." They could look in their big record book and give us information about my outfit that I didn't know, especially since I had come to the regiment late. They were really trying to fill in little gaps in their information. That first interrogation was not too severe and lasted only about an hour or less.

Our daily food ration was usually bread and a piece of cheese or some kind of preserved meat like sausage or salami. We had no mess kits, but I had my spoon, which I kept in my shoe top. Sometimes the bread was so hard and dry that we would run water over it before we ate it.

After four or five days, we were loaded onto the back of an open truck, all twenty-three of us. We started out after dark and soon we were riding in the light of a full moon. I sat on the edge of one side of the truck. One of the Italians was lying under my legs so that my legs were over him. As we were driving up and down, I could see a snow-covered peak from different views; it was beautiful in the moonlight. It represented a sparkling emerald. Suddenly an odor of a butter-flavored coconut cake seemed to fill my nostrils as though I were standing by the oven door when it came out. It did not seem unreasonable that a fully iced cake would come out of the oven. The odor almost overwhelmed me for a few seconds and then I began to smell something that seemed as though someone had gotten a shovel full of the filth out of an outhouse. This terrible odor seemed to come and go with the changing breeze caused by the varying speeds of the truck.

After a while the narrow edge of the sideboard I was sitting on began to cut into my backside. I reached down and shook the Italian under me and asked him to move so I could sit down on the bed of the truck. He just wiggled his shoulders and grunted. I shook him again, and he responded the same way. So I just eased off the side and sat down on him in the middle of his back. He just kind of grunted again and moved a little bit. I rode on him the rest of our journey that night.

I would guess that it was about two in the morning when we came to a town and eased down a hill toward a bridge. The truck stopped at the near end of the bridge and there was much discussion. Finally, the truck began to back up and we stopped at the upper end of the town. After some delay, the twenty-three of us were herded into a single room in an apartment building. The room was empty except for a single drawer from a wardrobe or dresser, lying upside down in the middle of the floor.

The only door was the one we entered. There was a single light bulb hanging in its socket by its two wires from the ceiling. We had to knock on the door to get permission from the guard outside in order to answer the call of nature. Outside we seemed to be down a pathway that led to the street if we went left; to the right was a sloping reed-covered bank to a river.

As soon as we were all in the house and the door was shut, my ex truck seat began to undress. He first took off his coveralls. Then he removed seven undershirts and seven pairs of shorts. The last thing he removed was the last pair of shorts, which were loaded with secondhand food. I then understood the source of that terrible odor. My erstwhile seat continued by crudely folding his deposit into the last pair of shorts, and then he tried to wipe the remaining goo from his anatomy with those same shorts. He then put on the rest of the clothes that he had doffed. When he had buttoned up his coveralls, he placed the drawer over the loaded shorts and then sat down upon it and looked around with an innocent and peaceful expression. He could not understand what the African American brothers were saying about him because he spoke only Italian.

One of his countrymen began to wring and twist with the urgency of his need to urinate. He was afraid to knock on the door to get permission from the guard to go out. Some of the brothers noticed his hesitancy because he went to the door and poised his fist to knock but hesitated because a brother would say, "Uh uh!"

He would put his hand down, move away from the door, and then begin to wring and twist with the urgency. After two such attempts that so amused our guys, I told him in Italian to knock and he would not be hurt or harmed by the guard.

When I eventually had to go out to relieve myself, the lack of "music roll" (toilet paper) presented a dilemma. There was snow. There was also rough, dried, brown cattail leaves that felt like sandpaper in your hands. I decided that I would use my thumb, which I would designate as the contaminated thumb and use my other hand to handle whatever food we should later receive. I proceeded to execute the process and then cleaned my thumb with snow.

When we finally received our first food in this one-room apartment, it had been about thirty-six hours since our last feeding. Our meal consisted of a slab of bread with a pat of white grease on top. When I looked at the bread and realized that I had to spread that grease (margarine) with my thumb, I forgot which thumb was the clean one. I struggled in myself with the debate for a few minutes. Then I finally took a chance, spread the grease on the bread, and ate it. The next time you go to the bathroom, thank God for simple blessings like toilet paper.

We spent several days in this apartment and here they began to process us as prisoners. They interrogated us again, this time a little more severely. They searched us again and we had to give up anything that was made of metal. Our helmets didn't go yet.. Those who had taps on their shoes had to remove them. We had to surrender our watches because they said that we could use a watch as a compass to assist an escape. They gave each man a receipt for his watch but they advised that it would be best if we would let them buy them from us. They hinted that the receipt did not mean we would get the same watch back; we would most likely get a watch that had belonged to someone who had made a beachhead and his watch had been full of saltwater. One of the buffalos had a twenty-one-jewel gold watch that he had received for his birthday a few months before. He sold it for seventy German cigarettes. The German cigarettes were rolled in brown paper and I have seen them burn on one side so that the burning part would reach the lips while the other half of the cigarette was still full length.

· · ·

CHAPTER 11
The Red Schoolhouse

After several days in the apartment, we were loaded onto a truck one night. We traveled to a brick building that had been a three- or four-room schoolhouse. This was the first heated building that we had been in. Thus far, our accommodations had been above freezing at night. We had our body heat, but we could never get comfortable enough for sitting or sleeping. Our hands and feet were always cold.

In the schoolhouse, it was warm and we had straw to sleep on. The schoolhouse was used as a collecting point for prisoners. When we arrived, there were British, other buffalos, and some white Americans. My wounds were treated by a medic corporal the next day. He used a probe in my hip wound and it brought out two or three more pieces of metal and some pus. The flesh had turned white by this time. A day or so later a lieutenant who spoke perfect English interrogated me. I determined to answer only my name, rank, and serial number. I said to myself that, no matter what, I would tell him nothing else at that session. He told me that if I didn't answer his questions I would not be taken to the hospital and, from the looks of my wounds, I would die. I still determined to answer him nothing. I said to myself that if he dismissed me and called me back in that I might answer him at that second session, but in this session, no answers. He kept asking me who my company commander was. This was the first time anyone questioned me alone. The other times we were questioned in the presence of the whole group. After about twenty minutes, he clapped his hands and a guard came and escorted me back to where the rest of the men were. A day or so later, after dark, men were loaded into trucks and taken away. When they filled all the trucks, four of us had to wait until the next night for another truck. The next day it snowed. It snowed for four days straight. After dark on the night of the fourth day, four of us were loaded into the back of a covered truck before five German soldiers who were going home on leave. The four days we had waited proved to be very boring because one of us had been singing two lines of a song, woefully out of tune, forty or fifty times every day. "Long may our land be bright, with freedom's holy light."

That seemed to be the only music he knew.

My feet were swollen again so this time I put on my shoes without my socks. We were in a covered truck and could see nothing of where we were going. We had only a small view out of the back. It turned cold that night, one of the coldest nights in Italy that year. When we walked on the snow, it sounded like dry sand under our feet. I have since figured out that it was less than 15° F. My feet got cold, and then became numb, and the numbness crept upward to my knees.

During the ride the truck started, stopped, and ground its way up hills and down. I could detect that we went down an incline onto a barge or ferry, and then crossed a body of water. I surmised that it was the Po River.

Four of us were finally unloaded inside a prison compound at something like 1:00 a.m. I took off my helmet and scooped it full of snow before I went inside, so I could use it to massage my feet back to life in the morning. We were ushered inside a huge empty warehouse. There was a pile of straw in the center of the floor and in one corner were three or four double-decker bunk beds. German bunk beds consisted of a ladder-like contraption with flat rungs. The three-inch-wide boards were placed about a foot apart. The mattress consisted of how much of our blankets we could put under ourselves. At this time, we were issued four blankets and instructed to avoid the straw pile. We were told that the straw pile was infested with lice. We were also told that we had a half an hour to select our bunks, make our beds, and get into them. I decided for the straw pile because it promised the most warmth. I had scooped up some snow in my helmet so that I could massage my frozen feet with it the next morning. As soon as the door was shut, the lights went out. I headed for the straw pile in the pitch darkness then I made a cocoon with my blankets and went to sleep. When I woke up the next morning, the snow was undisturbed in my helmet. My feet were still numb from the knees down.

We were ordered to go to a small building, also with no heat, and ordered to disrobe. Our clothes were to be treated in a special chamber to delouse them. Then we were to take cold showers with no towels. When I started to undress, the guard noticed my bandages, and told me to put my clothes back on. The other three guys who took those cold showers had almost become giant "goose pimples," and had to jump around after their showers to get dry and to keep from freezing. I thanked God for my bandages! A few minutes later, I was told to go outside and get in the back of a wagon pulled by a team of horses. There was some straw in the bottom of the wagon and I had a most pleasant ride on my back, looking up at the electric wires and the upper stories of buildings, and seeing the snow on the wires and the insulators on the telephone poles. The hospital was only about three miles from the prison camp. It was now the middle of January or later. I had not washed my face since I had been hit and now had more than a half-inch of beard. The right side of my face still had bits of dried blood in the beard.

· · ·

CHAPTER 12
The Hospital – Finally

I was helped out of the back of the wagon and told to enter the door of a building, which I later learned had been the children's hospital. When I got inside in the wide hallway, an orderly motioned me to enter a room with a sign over the door, "Camera Obscura," which meant "Dark Room." I thought I was to be X-rayed, but when I opened the door and entered the room, it turned out to be a small ward. It seemed crowded with the four beds that were in it.

A nun was teaching the occupants how to recite the Lord's Prayer in Italian. She would say a phrase and wait for them to repeat it after her. They were slaughtering that language so badly that I thought they must be from Brazil or someplace where the people spoke Portuguese! They were brown skinned, with uncombed, nappy hair, all tangled with bed lint.

When the prayer was finished, the nun looked at me and asked, "Ho fame?" "Are you hungry?" I replied, "Ci!"

She left and, while she was gone, the three black foreigners looked at me, and I looked back at them. They later told me that I was slightly bent over and looked to be at least forty years old with the growth of beard. When the nun returned with a bowl of warm soup, I took it in both hands, tipped it up to my lips, and drank it dry. One of the "foreigners" then said, "That n——r sure was hungry!"

Then I realized that they were from my own division, more African American buffalos.

A British orderly came and had me undress, the first time my clothes had been off since before Christmas. He picked me up in his arms and put me into a bathtub of warm water. My numb feet and legs began to ache and hurt, but the more pain I felt the more I rejoiced, because they would not hurt if they were frozen and dead. I had frostbite only on the tips of two or three toes on each foot. Those tips later became black and dropped off.

I found that I had two envelopes of sulfa powder in my shirt pocket. I then poured the powder into the wound in my upper leg, which by now was white inside. The sulfa powder quickly killed enough bacteria so that the flesh became a healthy pink in a day or so as the healing began. The healing process was so intense that it produced a terrible itching sensation, which I could not scratch.

Meanwhile, life in the hospital continued. The war seemed far away, even though we could hear bombs every once in awhile. The doctors and nurses were Italian. The nun acted the part that a nurse's aide would today. I don't know whether she cooked the food or not, but she often brought it to us. She and I became friends and I had many conversations with her. Every morning and evening temperature, pulse, and respiration readings (TPR) were taken and recorded. The thermometers were centigrade; thus, a healthy reading was 37°. They took temperature readings in our armpits and, due to the infrequency of baths and the total absence of deodorant, the thermometers had a certain aroma to them! They boiled and reused bandages. To this day, I believe the color of hospital green scrubs was inspired by the color of those secondhand bandages!

The sister (nun) and I shared many pleasant experiences. She would bring her friends, who had never seen a black person in their lives, to visit us. I was as much amused by them as they were by us. They would be talking about our hair, our color, and trying to surmise our birthplaces. They were always certain that we had come from Africa. After a while, I would start talking to them in Italian, and they would get excited and start asking me all kinds of questions. I would have to tell them to slow down and then explain to them that we were from the United States. One time, I told some of them that I was from Detroit, and they wanted to know how Henry Ford was the last time I saw him.

One day one of them decided to wash a brother's hands. At first, she gently scrubbed the palm of his hand, and said, "Fa polito." (It is getting clean). Then she scrubbed the back of his hand, and said, "No fa polito." (It won't get clean.) Meanwhile, he was softly calling her all kinds of unmentionable, four-letter names under his breath. They couldn't understand each other, and there was no harm done.

Medicines were in short supply. One of the guys had been shot through his foot. The foot became infected, and the doctors decided to amputate it. No one notified the foot owner of this decision. If he was told, the Italian did not get translated into English in his mind. The anesthesia was in short supply so that when they returned him to his bed right after the operation, he was awake enough to help lift himself onto the bed. The next day, he was lying on his back and decided to turn over. As he lifted his leg, the leg went way up in the air, because his muscles were not familiar with the absence of the weight of the foot. He stared at his leg for what seemed a full minute as he became conscious that his foot was missing. Then he turned to the wall and sobbed like a baby. His lament, which he cried over and over, was that he could never dance again.

The orderlies (ward boys) in the hospital were prisoners, mostly British. The head orderly was from South Africa. The "camera obscura" was his practice of apartheid (South African racial prejudice). When the nun asked for me to be her assistant as part of the hospital staff, she was unequivocally refused. Thus, I was deprived of a plush berth in which to wait out the end of the war.

· · ·

CHAPTER 13
My First Prison Camp

After about two and a half weeks, I was deemed healed and fit to return to prison camp. Two of us were loaded on a truck and transported back to the camp. The camp was nearly deserted then. Other prisoners had been shipped to Austria by train. At our first apel (an assembly in formation, so that prisoners could be counted), there were only five American, and maybe ten other prisoners in the entire camp. Of those five Americans, two were African American and three were white. We had to line up every morning and every evening by fives to be counted, British first, then the Americans, then the Commonwealth nations, then the French, then the Italians, and several other groups and finally, the Russians. Any officers were in formation after all the EM (enlisted men) were counted. When the population increased slightly, the Americans were separated by color. The white Americans were counted first, and then the African Americans. Six or eight weeks later, we ended up with twenty-two African Americans. At that time, there were fifty or sixty British, almost the same number of white Americans, then the twenty-two of us African Americans.

Then the numbers grew, so that every other Allied nation that fought on our side seemed to be represented. This included two Zulus from South Africa, a Senegalese from North Africa, and, of course, many others.

There were many other strange, POWs. One was a group of Sikhs from India. They were Nazirites, meaning that they did not cut their hair or shave. All of them had long black hair and flowing beards. Later, when some American butter found its way into our camp, they used it to comb their hair. Getting near one of them made me hungry every time, because that buttery aroma reminded me of hot biscuits, fresh bread, cake, and pie!

The Russians were treated differently. Because Russia had not signed the Geneva Convention, some of these prisoners had a type of trustee status. Certain ones were permitted to go into town and trade for bread. The currency they used was cigarettes—often American cigarettes—and sometimes British cigarettes.

So when the camp became overpopulated, we would line up in columns of five: the British first, next white Americans, then black Americans. Next in the line were Australians, New Zealanders, Afrikaners, French, Italians, Russians, and any other enlisted groups. Finally, the officers were counted. I don't know how they were organized, because I could not see that far away. We were counted every morning and every evening.

Some mornings, we had to turn out with our folded blankets. I think they just wanted to examine the blankets. Our beds consisted of two wooden pieces, two by fours by six feet long. These pieces were joined by five or six crosspieces that looked like the flat rungs of a ladder, nailed about a foot apart. Our mattresses, sheets, pillows, and blankets were the four blankets, that each of us was issued. Three of my four blankets were so small that I could hold them under my chin and my toes would show at the bottom.

We were housed in a large warehouse with concrete floors and a few windows on the front wall. The walls were made of square cement blocks. Our beds were either upper or lower bunk beds.

When my buddy and I first arrived at the almost deserted camp, it was cold—it was February. So we would wrap ourselves in the eight blankets because we had to have as many under us, as on top of us. Invariably, one of us would turn during the night, and totally destroy our bed. We would wake up cold in the morning. The only way to get warm was to go outside and walk up and down. At the same time, we were hungry and didn't have that much energy. So our hands and feet stayed cold most of the time. Since we were locked in the barracks after the evening count, our restroom facilities consisted of the bottom third of a fifty-five-gallon oil drum, with a handle on each side. It was someone's duty to empty this grand "slop jar" every morning. My turn came one morning, when there were ten to fifteen gallons of urine, and solid waste. The one who was holding the other handle permitted us to walk to the toilet house without any spills. But somehow or other, in the process of pouring it out, my forearm became baptized in the contributions of many men. I could only rinse it, outdoors, in cold running water. We had no soap, washcloths, or towels. We slept in all of our clothes, except our shoes. We discovered that after being unwashed for about two weeks we no longer stank. In other words, we got used to the odors.

Breakfast consisted of ersatz coffee. Since we were so cold, I would drink my coffee so hot that it would burn all the way to my stomach. It did seem to add a little heat to my body. After breakfast, we had to do calisthenics or some other form of exercise. The purpose of the exercise, we were told, was to help our breakfast get down to the proper places in our stomachs. The prison population continued to grow as prisoners were added from day to day. Later, we finally ended up with twenty-two black Americans in the camp. We would do close order drill for our morning exercise. I have to admit that we were pretty good at it. Usually we would command a viewing audience. "Goon" was the official title of a German guard. The goons told us that the exercises were designed to help our breakfast to digest better.

Our next meal was the biggest meal of the day. When it was time to eat, we were ordered to line up by threes, fours, or fives. The number indicated how many men would share a loaf of bread.

I must say something about this bread. I understand that the flour was ground from pine cones and chestnuts. It seemed to be rolled in sawdust before it was baked. Bread is considered to be the staff of life. Moreover, this bread was a real staff of life, because you could lean on a loaf, and it would support you without a denting! It was delivered to us on a wagon pulled by a team of horses, and it was stacked up like bricks. Since we were perpetually hungry, the driver had a long whip, which he used to keep us away from the wagon. A German soldier would be stationed on a bicycle about a hundred feet behind the wagon. This was to prevent someone from snatching a loaf of bread from the rear. The whip was not very effective at the rear of the wagon.

The guard on a bicycle was there to catch anyone who was able to snatch a loaf from the rear. To successfully steal a loaf of bread required teamwork. The one who grabbed a loaf would trot past a brother, and pass the loaf to him. But he would keep on trotting into the barracks, followed by the cyclist who would apprehend a thief with no bread. One of our newly arrived buffalos decided to get a loaf of bread as a solo effort, and the bicycle guard caught him. He spent seven days in solitary confinement.

Along with the bread we would receive the soup of the day—almost a quart of hot liquid. The first two days that I was in that camp, it seemed as though I had too much to eat. But by the third day, I began to be hungry, and the pangs of hunger did not leave me until a month after I was liberated. Because the soup was mostly water with very little substance, our urinary tracts became very healthy—while the rest of our system starved. The most common soup, which we called hedgerow soup, consisted of a greenish-looking water with a few leaves floating near the top. We surmised that the cook drove his team through the hedge-bordered lanes and picked a few leaves as he went by. Every now and then, there would be a little "essence" of meat in the soup. One day, just before lunch, I watched the cook use a big iron hook, which looked like a bailing hook to me, into the pot and pull out a horse's skull. Our soup tasted better and seemed to be more nourishing that day!

Sometimes, they would grind up beans and make them into a soup that would be so thick a spoon could stand up in the middle of it. But we still felt hungry after we ate. For suppers we got half as much bread, and no soup.

After a week or so, our hunger was ever present, leading us to think and dream and talk about food. We would describe to each other what we were going to eat when we got home. One brother collected recipes on sheets of the brown toilet paper. I said sheets, but the paper did not come in sheets—it came on a roll. When toilet paper ran out, his recipes had to go the way of all good toilet paper.

The British were the old-timers. They had been captured before Italy had capitulated, and they told us that when we came to ourselves we would quit talking about food. After a while, we learned that talking about food did make us hungrier. And so we became wise, as they were. But before we became wise we made a plan. There were four of us, and we decided that after liberation, we would get off the ship in New York Harbor and assemble in a restaurant. This is what we proposed to eat. We would each order our favorite pie. We would cut each pie into four pieces, then layer the pieces in a bowl with ice cream between each layer. A layer of ice cream on the top, covered with crushed pieces of chocolate-covered cherries would come next, and all of that would be covered with genuine whipped cream as a topping. We never had the opportunity to try that recipe.

Every now and then, Red Cross parcels would come through. Each Red Cross box was designed to supplement the diet of one prisoner for a week. During our stay in Italy, we had to divide a single parcel among four prisoners. And because of the constant disruption of rail service by the Allies, we got only about three parcels during our stay in Italy. Each American parcel contained, among other things, a box of Sun Maid raisins, a half pound of sugar, some tea, some sea biscuit crackers, a pound of butter in a can, one six-ounce Hershey bar, and five to seven packages of cigarettes. It would take us over two hours to divide a parcel among the four. For instance, we would count the raisins by twos into four piles. Then, after we had the four piles, one person would turn his back, while somebody else would point to a pile, and a third person would call a name. The hardest part was to divide the six portioned Hershey bar into four equal portions. The cigarettes usually went to those who smoked, even though cigarettes were treated as money. (More about "spending" cigarettes later.) Another problem presented itself in that if one tried to save some of his portion to eat on another day, the goons would declare a barracks inspection the following day, and confiscate any little bits of food that they found stored. So you took a chance on losing any food that you tried to save for another day.

And so life went on, and the prison camp slowly filled with freshly captured troops. Soon it became warm enough for us to spend time in the sun, taking our clothes off to kill the lice in the seams of our shirts and underwear.

We also had to fight bedbugs. When we got up in the morning, the bedbugs would have retired from our bodies into the crevices and joints of the wooden frames of our bed in order to digest their meal of the night before. We would take our wooden bed frames and stamp them on the floor to jar the bedbugs off. The floor would become covered with them, and we would walk on them and mash them with our shoes until the floor became slippery with blood. When we quit stomping them, the survivors would walk to the wall, climb up the wall, and take the same number of steps out on the ceiling to place themselves exactly over the middle of our beds, and then drop back down on our beds. One brother claimed that he watched an individual bedbug and counted the steps that it took to reach the wall from the middle of a bed. Then that same bedbug would climb the wall to the ceiling. And then he would carefully count the same number of steps from the beginning of the ceiling until he was in position to drop onto the same bed when it got dark. One night I was awakened by a tugging and a moving of my foot. I finally realized that a rat was gnawing on the nail of my big toe. I shook him off, pulled the blanket back over my foot, and went back to sleep. He must not have liked the flavor of my big toenail because he never bothered me again.

The official German term for prisoner of war was kreigenfanganen. And so we are known until this day as kreigies. One day, one of the kreigies managed to kill a rat. About fifteen of us stood in a circle around the dead rat and seriously debated whether we should ask the cook to put him in the stew. We were serious. We were not joking or making wisecracks. We finally decided that the germ count would be too high and probably would make us sick. On another day, one of the goons was carrying a sack of hog feed through the yard, dropped it, and it broke open. He left it lying there. We scooped up handfuls of it and mixed it with our next serving of soup.

Three barbed wire fences each about ten to twelve feet high surrounded our entire camp. The innermost fence was spaced five or six feet from the next fence. The guards walked back and forth in this space. Every so often, there was a little hut, just big enough for a guard to stand in during inclement weather. Between Fence Number Two and Fence Number Three were loose coils of barbed wire. The back wall of our barracks was located on the shore of a lake. After our evening apel, we would be locked into the barracks for the night. As our population grew, we received some experienced prisoners who had been recaptured after the Italian capitulation. They began to plan ways and means of escape. Every night we would entertain one another with singing. The first night the British would sing. The next night the Americans would sing. And then, the French, the Commonwealth nations, the Italians, and others would sing in their turn. Sikhs, the people from India who never cut their hair or shaved, and had long black hair and beards, rendered the music that was hardest to bear. Their singing sounded like a mournful wail with no beginning or ending. There was simply a continued wailing, mournful sound.

The singing helped to cover up the noise of one of our unsuccessful escape attempts. Some of the blocks in the back wall were removed and dirt was removed to form the beginning of a tunnel. A line would form and each man in turn would have a pocket filled with dirt. When we had done enough digging for the night, we placed blocks back in the wall with a mortar formed from soap and sand. It was impossible to see where the blocks had been removed. The next day the men with the dirt in their pockets would quietly empty their pockets out in the yard when no one was looking. The tunnel was supposed to take us under the barbed wire and just above the lakeshore line. I decided that if I had a chance to go through the tunnel, I would attempt to make an escape. At that time, it seemed as though the Italian populace was 9-1 pro-Allies. Since I could speak the language fairly well, I thought I might have a good chance of being hidden by friendly Italians and being able to escape to Allied lines. I was strengthened in this resolve by the appearance among us of a Senegalese soldier who had been captured much earlier; he had escaped at the Italian capitulation. He had lived with an Italian family in a mountainous village for more than a year.

One day a new American prisoner arrived. They counted him in the evening apel with the white Americans and locked him in with us that night. The next day he walked over to one of the goons and said something to him. Soon the camp commandant, with a small entourage, walked into the barracks. They went to the back wall. The commandant, using his swagger stick, pushed a block in and exposed the tunnel. After that, singing was prohibited.

A couple of hours after our tunnel was discovered, a German staff car arrived at the gate. Our new prisoner of the day before was let out of the gate, got in the staff car, and left. In other words, he was a German who spoke perfect English and he was planted to discover our business.

A short time later, a British paratroop major arrived at the camp as a new kreigie. He was educated at Oxford and very interesting to talk to. He told me that he had been dropped by parachute into enemy territory in order to organize and facilitate the work that the partisans were doing. And, when he settled to the ground in his parachute, he landed in a squad of Germans who were sitting around eating their evening meal! Of course, he ended up in prison camp.

About this time, after an abortive attempt to place us in boxcars and transport us to Germany, the guards decided to organize some kind of recreational activity or program. The British major persuaded me to organize a four-member spelling team to participate in a spell down. I had a hard time getting the guys to agree to participate. And I assured them that they would have to spell only small, everyday words. We were to face another team in a spelling bee. Finally four of us arrived in front of an audience and faced our opponents for the first word. I don't remember what that first word was, but when it was pronounced, the three guys all looked at me. I told them that this was just the first word, and it would get better. The second word was "daguerreotype."

Those three guys looked at me, threw up their hands, and walked away. That was the end of the spelling bee. An amateur singing contest fared much better. In fact, a African American quartet won first prize, appropriately singing the song, "I Don't Get Around

Much Anymore." An Irish tenor solo won second prize. His prize turned out to be twice as much as each first-prize winner received. That prize was a loaf of bread that had to be split four ways. The second prize was half of a loaf of bread—with no splitting!

Our population grew until there were over four hundred men in the camp. There was a library with a few books in it. There were two complete decks of cards. One deck was used in a perpetual bridge game, and the other deck was used in a perpetual whist game. Even though I had been taught all my life that card playing was a sinful pastime, I decided that since there was no money to be bet, I would learn to play bid whist. My mentor was a grade school dropout from Mississippi—but he was a card shark. We became champions, which meant that we would play game after game and beat all challengers. Then there were days when we could not win any game.

Later, after I finally got home, I found out that I was expert in playing the popular game rook. Soon afterward, I decided that this was card playing for me, after all, and I stopped playing rook in 1948.

And so life went on. About April 12 or 13, 1945, two German soldiers who could speak English, brought another buffalo prisoner into camp. He was rather tall, dark skinned, muscular, and not very bright. These two German guards had escorted him from place to place as an "exhibit" in a cage to display that African Americans were half apes. And since he did not understand what they were saying about him and many of the Germans who saw him had never seen a black man before, he enjoyed himself. He was displayed in the cage and touted as an ape man. The women were especially curious, and would come and touch him to see if his color would rub off on them, and feel his muscles.

But those two guys who brought him back to camp had some news to share with us that they thought was wonderful. They announced the death of President Roosevelt. To them this meant that we were going to lose the war. I remember telling one of them that I was from Detroit and that we were rolling out war materials faster than they could destroy them. I mentioned that at Willow Run, B-24 Liberator bombers rolled off the assembly line every fifteen minutes.

The goon who came closest to being able to communicate with us was more than six feet tall and had been in the Afrika Corps. He sometimes wore the shorts that were part of the official German uniform in North Africa. He was the one who would make announcements or pronounce sentence upon those who needed to be punished. I remember the sentence he pronounced upon someone who had stolen a loaf of bread: "It is strictly verboten to stolling one loaf of bread!"

Our private name for him was "Big Stooper."

The goon corporal who counted us every day was a little less than average height and much smaller in size. His every move was the personification of military bearing. He wore boots almost to his knees that shined with a mirror finish. He would march to the front of each group, come to a halt, do a right face, and then begin to count. He would march to the front and center of each successive group and begin to count us in German. On two different occasions when he was counting either the white Americans or the black Americans, somebody in the British ranks broke wind with a very loud and gurgling sound. He flew into a rage, pulled his Lugar out of its holster, paced up and down, and filled the air with German curses. We remained at rigid attention. My stomach was tied in knots trying to keep from laughing. We didn't dare laugh, and no one ever got shot.

One afternoon, the British paratroop major whom I had befriended scaled the three fences while wearing a trench coat and disappeared. He picked the timing so that the guards who were in sight of the place that he scaled were all walking away from him. He had told the lieutenant whose trench coat he borrowed that he had been dropped to perform a mission and it was time for him to accomplish that mission. Only a few of the kreigies who happened to be lying on the ground sunning themselves saw the amazing feat with their own eyes. He seemed to scale the barbed wire fences as easily as a cat running up a tree. The trench coat proved to be no hindrance. Within ten minutes, every kreigie knew. The goons did not discover the escape until the evening apel.

The evening count was routine until they counted the officers. Then came a blowing of whistles, shouting of commands, and searching to no avail. We knew that the escape was successful because, if they had caught him, they would have paraded him in front of us to show us that we couldn't escape. After that, they counted us three times a day.

• • •

CHAPTER 14
Prison Trains to Germany

Our captors finally decided to make a prisoner shipment to Germany. We had to line up to be strip-searched. In the space where the searching went on were two big boxes. As one would begin to put his clothes back on, he would be instructed to discard certain pieces into one of the boxes. I was allowed to keep all of my clothes since most of them were full of holes and blood stains. Then we were marched to a railroad siding and loaded into the 32/8 or 40/8 boxcars. The numbers, 32/8 or 40/8 meant that the capacity of the car was thirty-two or forty men or eight horses. We were packed in the 32/8 cars fifty, fifty-one, or fifty-two men, and then the doors were closed. Each car had a square wooden box, almost three feet on a side, with three or four inches of sand in the bottom. That was our solid waste commode. Since we were all males, liquid waste had to be aimed through the cracks in the doors. Woe be unto you if you could not differentiate as to which kind of waste you were producing at a time. There was not room for all of us to sit down, much less to lie down, and so a great number of us would have to stand up. The first twenty-four hours locked in a boxcar were really miserable. I remember standing over a small British soldier who was sitting with his back to the wall and I was leaning on the wall over his head. Part of our discussion had to do with the differences between American English and Oxford English. Then the brother passed some vociferous and malodorous gas. His explanation was that there was more room out then there was in. There was no room for one to move to escape the aroma.

By the second night, we finally learned how that we could all lie down to sleep. Each had to lie with his head to the side wall. And since his feet would be up on the legs of the men on the other side we had to take our shoes off. That's when I understood how Jacob took a stone for a pillow, because I slept with my shoes for a pillow. All the men on one side had to face the same direction and the men on the other side would face the opposite direction. You could turn over during the night only if everybody on your side turned. We were jammed against each other so there was no room to turn or to move our arms or stretch our limbs. Often the train would be moving during the night but I could sleep through most of it.

It took us about two and a half weeks to make a journey that normally would have lasted about thirty-six hours. We spent one week in a small town that had been part of Germany after World War I. So the town had a German and an Italian name, Brixen and Bressanone. We were sequestered in a house and its small backyard. The backyard was limited by two tables, end to end, on each side. The German guards were stationed outside the tables. And they would conveniently look away when Italians would place food on the tables for us. I saw one of the two Zulus receive a small loaf of bread. One of the big blue-eyed blond Afrikaners walked up to him and just took the bread as though it belonged to him. I told my sergeant, and he said, "Two of you back me up."

He walked up to the Afrikaner, grabbed the front of his shirt, and looking up at him, made him give the bread back to the Zulu and watch him eat it. The Zulu was so nervous that he choked on the bread. The Afrikaner's face turned red and white like a neon sign. But he did not move. There were nine of them. There were twenty-two of us African Americans.

Another day in the boxcars was spent on a track in a railroad marshaling yard. There was a string of tank cars four tracks over from us. At one time during that day, two American fighter planes decided to strafe the tank cars. We knew that our boxcars had big POW and red crosses on their roofs. We also knew that Germans would use these markings to camouflage their trains carrying war materials—so we expected to be strafed. We were literally shaking with fear. A white boy from Texas was lying directly behind me and he squeezed me in his arms as he shook. The fear produced so much adrenaline that we could smell it.

I was not afraid and I thought I would say something amusing to relieve the tension. One of my friends, whom I still correspond with today, threatened to hit me because he said "It is sacrilegious to joke at a time like this." Remember, we were in boxcars and could not see what was happening outside but we could hear it.

One of the Sikhs had used a turban to conceal a trench knife. A turban is a piece of cloth about four inches wide and thirteen feet long. Even though I watched the act, I still don't know how they do it, but they put one end on their head and start winding. They tuck in the other end and it is done. Anyway, one of them concealed a trench knife in his turban and it was not discovered when he was strip-searched. The kreigies in that car managed to carve a square hole in the floor of their boxcar. When the train was stopped in a valley and the goons were more or less in a bunch, smoking and talking, three men managed to escape through the hole in the floor. The first one started climbing up through the wooded slope that ended at the top of the valley. The second man was shot just before he got to the woods. We stayed in that valley all day. Toward evening, an SS trooper brought the British soldier back to the train. The train commandant took off his belt and beat the prisoner with the buckle end, striking him on the head and in the face. Every goon belt buckle I saw had "Got Mit Uns" engraved or printed on it. The beaten man was put into our car after his beating. He had climbed most of the day until he got to a road. He saw two houses and he had to take a chance that they were not Fascist. A young woman came to the door of the first house and welcomed him to come in. Her boyfriend was an SS trooper.

. . .

CHAPTER 15
Arrival at Stalag 7A

We spent our last night locked in the boxcars in the city of Munich. The British mounted one of their nighttime air raids. We could hear the bombs falling and exploding. There were a few dogs howling. Most of the dogs and cats that were not closely guarded pets had been eaten by this time. The next day we arrived at Stalag 7A.

At this time, there were approximately 160,000 prisoners in this camp. As the Russians and the allies advanced, more and more prisoners were concentrated in Stalag 7A and other such camps. That first day, we were lined up and issued a British Red Cross parcel for every two men. My Mississippi buddy and I shared a parcel. We were given about seven packages of cigarettes on the side, because the British did not put cigarettes in their parcels. We also received a can of Argentina bulk. Argentina sent cases of canned beef stew. We each got a can of stew. So we ate the stew and we mixed about half of the dehydrated eggs and ate that. Even though our stomachs were full, we still felt hungry, and that was not all that we ate that day.

That afternoon I saw a Russian soldier wearing a long heavy wool coat. I indicated to him that I would like to trade his coat for my field jacket. And so we began the trading process. We both knew how to count in German. That was the only language that we had in common. At first, he wanted my field jacket plus fifty-five cigarettes. About three hours later, I had the coat and he had my field jacket and fifteen cigarettes. Later that evening I met a Greek soldier who told me that he had an empty bunk in his bunkhouse. So I left my buddy outside to sleep on the ground under the coat that covered him almost like a tent. After the Greeks finished a game of cards, I crawled into a bunk and prepared to sleep. A few minutes later, the single lightbulb was turned back on because somebody had forgotten something. When the light was on, I saw a big brown spot, almost a foot in diameter, moving on the wall toward my bunk. It was a solid mass of bedbugs moving in for their nightly feast. I went outside and got under the coat with my buddy. There was a soft drizzly rain falling.

Soon another problem became evident. The combination of foods that we had eaten that day began to generate various and sundry gases. Those gases made the space under the coat untenable. So we ended up walking up and down in the rain for the rest of the night. The next day we got separated and I was assigned to a large tent that held seventy-two kreigies; I was the only African American. All the rest were white Americans.

A tech sergeant named Curly was more or less in charge. Each day, everyone contributed a cigarette. They were presented to the guard with the assurance that all were present and accounted for, and we did not have to fall out for apel. Here as many as twelve men received only one loaf of bread. Sometimes the bread would be green with mold. We did not try to brush it off because it would waste too much of the bread. Sometimes our meal, besides the bread, would be two small boiled potatoes. Some days we got a little bit of sauerkraut. That is when I came to the realization of why the Germans were called Krauts.

Twice we received a small piece of Limburger cheese. That cheese smelled like it had been dead, without refrigeration for a month. You could not eat it without that terrible odor getting into your nostrils. We tried holding our noses, holding our breath, but nothing worked. Even so, we were too hungry not to eat it.

Some of the kreigies were housed in long bunkhouses that had stoves in them. Some of the men, especially the British, had been prisoners for almost five years. Somehow, radios had been smuggled into the camp in pieces. These were radios with tubes in them because transistors were not yet developed. These were carefully disassembled, then dismantled, and hidden in the ash places in the stoves. Each evening the radios were secretly assembled and tuned to hear the news from the BBC. After the news, the radios were disassembled and hidden once more. The three or four who had heard the news would each instruct three or four others who would spread the news so that an hour later all of us knew how close the

Americans were to us from one direction and the Russians from the opposite direction. And, as far as I know, the goons never caught on as to how we got the news.

Some of the prisoners had made a cooking apparatus called a blower constructed from tin cans. Each was equipped with a crank, which, when it was turned, would make even a few sticks of wood hot enough to cook whatever you could find to put in the pot. Some of the Russians still had the privilege of being able to go into town and buy food for cigarettes. We did get some more Red Cross parcel distributions in this place, so we had a small income of cigarettes, if we didn't smoke. Along one edge of our fenced in section, zigzag trenches had been dug and their sides shored up by green twigs or whips. We were supposed to take shelter in the trenches in case of an air raid.

We often saw American planes in the skies overhead during the day. Sometimes, at twilight, we would see German planes, but by this time, the Allies ruled the skies in the daytime. The German planes would fly only when the other planes had gone home. One evening, a German jet plane flew over. I heard it, but I never did see it because it was going so fast that my eyes seem to follow the sound instead of sighting the plane itself. It was also here that I saw some American heavy bombers making a low-level bombing run on a nearby town. It seemed as though the planes were heading straight toward us and I could see the bomb bay doors open and the bombs tumbling out. They seemed to seesaw as they headed toward the ground. Before those bombs hit, I was in the bottom of the trench, trying to get deeper. I heard the explosions but I did not see them.

We were praying that the Americans would get to us first. The Russian prisoners were ardently wishing for an American liberation because some of them would be executed for permitting themselves to become prisoners. They did not want to be liberated by their own countrymen.

• • •

CHAPTER 16
American Liberation! General Patton Comes to Camp!

About eight o'clock on a Sunday morning, April 29, 1945, we heard an artillery battle somewhere within two or three miles from our camp. We could recognize the sounds of American guns and German guns. We swarmed out into the streets, cheering. There were still dangers, however. A German officer fired his pistol down the street and one bullet ricocheted and hit an American in his knee. After a while, the battle drew very near. Then we dove into the trenches and behind buildings.

Then we saw an American tank, followed by a halftrack tank destroyer, loaded with soldiers, coming up to the main gate. They didn't bother to open the gate—they just ran over it and came into the camp! They stopped inside the camp, pulled the swastika down the flagpole, and then ran up the Stars and Stripes.

I cried, and knelt down and kissed the ground, and then I turned around and, lo, the camp was full of every kind of flag that represented every Allied nation. These had been secretly made and kept hidden until this moment! So from every barrack roof and tent pole, flags of all the Allied nations were flying. A few halftracks and trucks with troops began to roll through the camp. The guys asked if we were hungry.

We shouted, "Yes!"

So they began to throw us the K rations that they had stuffed in their shirts for emergencies. Each prisoner who received one tore it open and began to eat, starting at one end, eating until he got to the other end. The rescue troops exclaimed that we had to be hungry to eat K rations like that!

On Monday, General Patton walked through our camp with several officers of various ranks. He passed about six feet from where I was standing. He had only one of his trademark pearl-handled six-shooters that day.

That afternoon, many kreigies walked out of camp to search for food. I decided that I would wait one more day because I did not want to get picked off by any snipers left behind. The next day the liberators replaced the goon guards with American soldiers. They were stationed at every gate. If a prisoner wanted out, all he had to do was cut a hole in the fence to one side of the gate. When he returned, a guard would be stationed at that hole so he would have to cut a new hole to enter. I exited the camp at a newly cut unguarded hole.

As I walked, everywhere I turned I saw slaughtered sheep, pigs, and cows. Most of the carcasses had been expertly butchered. I came across an African American laundering company. They gave me a pair of shoes that fit my feet. They gave me some more food. They also gave me a pair of wire cutters because I would need them to get back into camp. The guards would not let us in the hole they were guarding, but would conveniently look away while we cut a new hole just a few feet away from the old one!

Back in the camp, kitchens were set up and we got in long chow lines to eat American food again. A chaplain who had a jeep and a trailer both loaded with food would come and park in a certain area. We would again form a long line. He might count three men in the line and hand them a loaf of bread. Or the next ten men would each get a candy bar. Whatever we got we would immediately devour it. I saw him count off nine men to whom he handed a gallon of peanut butter. They each got a spoon and took turns dipping into the peanut butter until it was all gone. Even though we ate everything that we could get our hands on, we still felt hungry.

One of my fellow buffalos had gone outside the camp looking for meat. He ended up harvesting the tongues out of the heads of the butchered animals that he came across. Tongues were a delicacy for him. When I saw him again he had tongues hanging out of his pockets. He had a blower going with a frying pan on it and he was frying those tongues. I saw some Russians who had brought a live pig into camp. They surrounded that pig and started slicing on him even before they cut his throat. He didn't squeal very long.

I bought a live chicken with some cigarettes and proceeded to slaughter, pluck, and dress it. I took the entrails out but forgot about the gallbladder. After it was cooked, it had a very bitter taste as I ate it. Of course, I ate it.

Nine or ten days later, we were finally transported out of Stalag 7A. Back in Italy, I had fashioned a hat out of the woolen shirt panel that had made the front of my shirt opening windproof. The hat even had a reinforced cardboard bill. I was seated facing backward in a 6 × 6, one of a long convoy of trucks heading toward a grassy meadow that was the landing strip for the C-3 cargo planes that were to fly us out. My head hit a low-hanging branch that gently removed my hat, and I lost it.

We finally arrived at the landing field and men were loaded into the planes by a priority based on their length of stay as kreigies. Some Britons there had been away from home for five years. Finally, it got too dark to fly and about twenty of us were left to spend the night in the open field. There was a huge pile of blankets, so we had no problem keeping warm at that time. The last meal that I ate on German soil consisted of a pound of powdered milk and a can of tuna fish. I ate the milk by the spoonful and then the tuna fish. I was told that a combination of fish and milk would kill a person but I've proved that to be a false premise. After I finished eating, I drank some water. Then my stomach began to bubble and gurgle and I seemed to be very full. But I still felt hungry. The next morning we were among the first to be loaded, and took off for France. Sitting in that noisy plane without any insulation, we were treated to the sounds of loudspeaker broadcasting VE Day, the end of the war in Europe. But the noise of the engines was so loud that we could not understand anything that was being said.

• • •

CHAPTER 17
Camp Lucky Strike

We finally landed and were trucked to Camp Lucky Strike. As we walked in line through the gates to a reception area, two young women who represented the Red Cross greeted us. They were passing out doughnuts, and they gave each of us only two doughnuts. I asked why, and one of them told me that the first prisoners they had greeted were allowed to eat as many donuts as they wanted. One ex-POW had eaten fifty-nine doughnuts and died the next day. So after that, our food was portioned out to us as though we were patients in a hospital on a restricted diet. Our food seemed to be semisoft and in limited supply. Here we were issued new clothes, but somehow I managed to keep the wool undershirt that I had worn ever since before Christmas.

We were interviewed and then given a form to sign stating that we wished to resume our American citizenship—since we had been the guests of a foreign country. We were each issued US $20. Then we boarded a ship. We left Le Havre, France, bound for Southampton, England. There was a PX on the ship and I bought $16 worth of candy and chewing gum. In the mess hall, our dieting was over, so I would eat two plates of food for each meal and one dozen candy bars. The candy bars were Baby Ruths and O Henrys that today cost about sixty-nine cents each, but at that time they were five cents each. We docked in a few hours at Southampton. We were not permitted to go ashore, so I just leaned over the rail and spit on Southampton.

Some troops who had been destined for Europe were on the dock, drawn up in formation with leggings on, only now they were going home. With their helmets strapped under their chins, these men had the general appearance of basic training recruits. We felt cheated that they were going home on the shame ship that we were, though they had never been shot at or starved in a prison camp. And so we began to make fun of them. We told them that they looked like Boy Scouts. We told them how pretty their uniforms were, and some other things that are not worth repeating. Many of them turned red in the face and some even began to cry. As soon as they got on board, they changed their clothes so they looked just like we did. That is when I began to understand the seriousness of the brotherhood of "them that got shot at."

That brotherhood still exists, and has existed, through all the wars and conflicts, including Iraq, to this day.

. . .

CHAPTER 18
Homeward Bound!

After three days at sea, I had eaten forty-eight candy bars. The voyage was pleasant at first because we could have lights on the ship, we didn't have to zigzag, and we didn't have to go below decks at night until we wanted to. But then, a storm blew up and the ship began to rock and to climb up and down the waves. One had the sensation of rising three floors and dropping three floors in a fast elevator. Only the elevator would not stop and let you off but would repeat the process day and night. I got so seasick that I lost all of my undigested food, and worse than that, I lost my appetite. For the first time in months, I did not feel hungry. Finally, after two days of storm, the sea calmed down and the next day we could see land in the distance. As the thin black line, which represented the distant shore, began to rise out of the water we could recognize New York Harbor. We passed by that beautiful lady, the Statue of Liberty. As we began to go up the East River, office buildings along the shore were throwing confetti out of their windows to greet us. Finally, we docked at Pier 45.

Soon after dark, we disembarked and boarded trucks that took us to Camp Shanks, New York. We were fed a meal of steak, mashed potatoes, gravy, and some other stuff. A photographer shot a picture of me with a piece of steak on my fork halfway up to my mouth. This picture appeared in the Negro press along with pictures of two of the Tuskegee Airmen who had been in the same prison camp. I later received a letter from a young woman in Florida who had seen those pictures. I have since had several conversations with the two Tuskegee Airmen even though I didn't meet them until more than thirty years later. (And that is another story!)

The next day I was on a train bound for the Great Lakes Naval Training Station outside of Chicago. After one or two days in Great Lakes, Illinois, I remember being in the train station in Chicago on a Friday night, looking for the track where I could catch the Michigan

Central bound for Detroit. I met a fellow soldier from Detroit, the first contact that I had had with anyone from Detroit, and now we were headed home!

We chatted for a few minutes. He was able to tell me that both of my parents were still alive. He also told me that the Lake Region Conference had conducted a regional camp meeting the weekend before. I was confused because the only conference that I knew was the Michigan conference and they had conducted all of their camp meetings at Grand Ledge.

He explained to me that a regional conference had been formed. That was the first time that I learned that a segregated conference could exist.

. . .

CHAPTER 19
Home at Last!

I boarded the train at about nine or ten that night and rode through the night. The train arrived in Detroit early enough for me to catch a taxi and knock on my front door before five in the morning.

I was finally home. It had been over fifteen months since I had left. I greeted Mom and Dad, but none of us realized that I still had the "front line" frame of mind. I was partially uncivilized. And I still remembered the vow that I had made, that I would not tell anyone any of the things that had happened to me because I didn't think they would believe it and if they didn't believe it, they would face dire consequences.

And so I would tell just a little bit and watch out of the corner of my eye to see if they believed it or not. When it came time to go to church and I was asked to say a few words, I told them how beautiful the mountains in Italy were with the full moon shining on them, but did not mention the hardships.

For some time, I had to sleep on the floor because the beds were too soft. One day when I was walking home from the car line, a little boy about five years old fired two cap pistols just as I was walking by. I immediately hit the ground. It seemed as though I realized in midair before my body hit the ground that I was not in a war zone anymore. So I never repeated that action.

My girlfriend, whom I had tearfully parted from fifteen months before, had not been very faithful, and my parents warned me that things were not the way they had been when I left. So I called her rather than going to see her in person and we had several lengthy conversations on the phone. We decided that we would meet at her church at the Missionary Volunteer meeting the next Sabbath to talk over our situation and to decide where we should go from there. I was afraid to face her because the sight of her might have melted all of my resolve. And so when I saw her outside of the West Side

Church just before MV meeting started, she was beautiful to behold. We started to talk and then one or two minutes later, a civilian called to her from across the street. She excused herself for a minute and walked out of my life forever.

It took me awhile to become civilized. I had made up my mind that I would say what ever came into my mind as long as it was the truth. A young woman who had heard about me came to Detroit to see me. When I met her, I told her, "You sure look ugly to me!"

Then I turned and walked away. My mother witnessed the action and she said that the girl's face almost melted in disappointment. I am so thankful that I didn't meet my wife during those first two or three years that I was home.

Actually, that first visit home was just a two-month delay en route, or a sixty-day furlough. After two weeks, I became bored, so I went to work on the job I had left when I got drafted. During World War II, it was against the law for someone in the service to wear civilian clothes at any time. So I had to wear my uniform for dress and my fatigues for work. I found now that I was the dean of forestry helpers for the city of Detroit. When I left, I was the first and only African American forestry helper in the history of the city.

After the sixty days, I reported to Hotel Dennis on the beach at Atlantic City, New Jersey. Here they removed that small piece of glass that had hidden in a pimple under my right eye. I took the AGCT test for the second time. I think I scored four points less than I did the first time I took it. I also received some back pay, more than $300. I remember walking on the boardwalk with three US $100 bills in my pocket and rubbing them together as I walked. That was the most money I'd ever had in my hands at one time in my entire life. I finally went to a Western Union office and wired the money home.

One morning, about twenty of us were sitting in one of the E and I (education and information) sessions. These sessions were intended to make enlisted men more intelligent. This particular morning when the instructor came in, he was bursting with enthusiasm. He had a newspaper with big screaming headlines, all about the atom bomb. This was on or about August 4, 1945. He began to "spout" and actually almost shout about the great achievement in that first bombing on Japan, and the tremendous force of the explosion. All of us sat and obediently listened. But in my own mind, I said, "So what?"

I think almost all of our minds were saying the same thing. Our teacher began to slow down and run out of steam. Finally he said, "Don't you guys care about this?"

One of the guys asked him in a very calm and matter-of-fact voice, "Have you ever been shot at?"

He paused just for a moment, then folded up his paper and quietly left.

• • •

.

CHAPTER 20
Final Army Days

After four days of Atlantic City and the boardwalk, I was shipped to Camp Crowder, Missouri, for rations and quarters. This meant that my sole mission until a change was made was to be fed and housed. I arrived at this camp and was assigned to an empty bunk in a one-floor barracks. At six o'clock in the morning a sergeant strode into the building, blew his whistle, and gave the usual call "Wakee wakee, rise and shine!"

I turned over and prepared to go back to sleep. In a few minutes, the sergeant returned and stood at the foot of my bunk and blew the whistle with his cheeks puffed out. I looked up at him and said, "I wish you would swallow that thing!"

Then I turned over again and went back to sleep. In a few minutes, I received a summons to report to the captain. After I dressed, I reported to the captain, and realized that I had met him two years before. I had devised a "jitterbug salute." In my mind, I proposed to use this salute until some officer stopped me. The strange thing was that no one stopped me and I saluted like that until I became a civilian, no longer required to salute officers. And so, that morning I gave the captain my jitterbug salute.

He told me in an apologetic voice that I was a part of a company of new recruits in their third week of basic training. So he asked me if I could get up when they did to keep from hurting their disciplinary training. I assured him that I would from then on.

I had no duties to perform except that one day, when I had gone on a three-day pass, I was assigned KP in my absence. So I did the KP that one time, even though placing my name on the roster was a mistake. I was still at this camp when VJ-day occurred. World War II was finally over, and we were restricted to the post. I didn't get to experience any of the victory celebrations that occurred all over the world!

A week or two later I was assigned for duty to the post hospital in Fort Bragg, North Carolina. My first assignment, the day after I arrived, was as a ward boy on the German POW ward. I walked through the ward and then announced that the ward was filthy—the windows needed washing, the floor needed to be scrubbed, and I was determined that all able-bodied men on *that* ward would perform those duties.

Within an hour, the charge nurse had called headquarters and asked them to please get that private off her ward because the men's temperatures were rising and they were becoming sick! I had told those men that I knew exactly how to treat them because of my own ample lessons from German prison camps.

The next day I was reassigned to duty as a chancre mechanic. The army had just begun to use penicillin to treat primary syphilis. The treatment consisted of a penicillin shot in the upper outer quadrant of the hip every four hours for five days. So I had to administer those shots three times to each patient during my daytime shift. In between times, I had to sharpen the needles and autoclave them. Then I had time to read, doze, or to visit around the hospital. After two or three days of treatment, the men's hips became very sore, even though I had become an expert at administering the shots with the least amount of pain. So I would often inquire, "Left behind?" or "Right behind?"

Forty years later, in light of my medic experiences, I was a little amused at discussions I heard about the "Rapture" and about those who would be "left behind." To me, the term "left behind" meant that you wish to be punctured in the upper outer quadrant of your left hip.

I was able to again get Sabbath off and to attend church in Fayetteville, North Carolina. The segregated bus that we would catch to go to town had abbreviated the words, colored troops, on the front of the bus. We termed the bus "Cool Troops." The bus reached the end of the line a little way past our barracks where it would turn around and come back. We would know to go out to catch the bus when we would hear the cry, "Cool troops in the hole."

One evening, after my shift, I was in the barracks where my bed was. I was handed a letter and a small black box. In it was a Purple Heart with my name on it. And so I received official notice and was awarded the medal that I had earned by being wounded due to enemy action. On another evening, one of the guys explained to us that he knew how to make conk, which was a greasy chemical hair straightener. It would make one's hair straight and silky. I had tried a commercial brand before I was drafted and the second time I used it, I got a little bit on my bare forehead. It burned my skin and left a little scar. I never used the stuff again. But this entrepreneur in the barracks said that he would give a free treatment to the first one to try out his concoction. And so he treated a brother's head. When he finished, the hair was indeed straight and black and silky. And so the brother put a stocking cap on. The next morning, when he pulled the stocking cap off, every single hair came with it. Those were the days when bald heads were extremely rare.

• • •

CHAPTER 21
Discharged!

I finally received a notice that I would be discharged in about a week. I had earned enough points so that I could get discharged early. The points were earned by one's length of stay in the army, one point per month. This became two points per month for each month spent overseas. One received five points for each battle star or campaign star. And I received five points for the Purple Heart. So by the end of October 1945, I had sixty-four points, enough to get discharged. About the first of November I was told that every ex-prisoner was to receive a stripe, which would have made me a Pfc. I reached out my hand and asked them to hand me the stripe. They said the paperwork would take about three days. I told them to keep the stripe. On November 4, 1945 I reported to the discharge center and joined the line of those who were being mustered out. I received my honorable discharge but the paper that went with it got mixed up with someone in front of me or behind me. It said that my highest MOS was basic rifleman, so I had no record of my combat medical experience or my qualification as a surgical technician. I was on my way home!

At this stage in my life, I was still uncivilized. The process of becoming civilized took me at least three years. The beginning of the process was during the two months' furlough that I had enjoyed when I arrived back in the States. I had worked on my old job for six weeks. During most of that time, I slept on the floor because the bed was too soft. I found that on my job I was treated somewhat special because at this time I was the dean of forestry helpers. The first day I was on the job I received a truck and a driver and sent to do a few odds-and-ends jobs at two or three playground lots. One of these was to rig a flagpole at a "tot lot." This meant that I had to climb the flagpole, hand over hand, with no ladder or any other help. I was not in the best physical condition. I was still underweight and had done no real exercise for a long time. But the young woman said that she "so wanted to fly the flag for the tots that she was caring for," and she was "so hoping that I could rig the pole for her."

I strained and stretched every muscle I had to get to the top of that pole and put a rope through.

My actual transformation into a civilian began after I was finally discharged in the early part of November 1945. I still had the mind-set of "one who has been shot at."

I received these in 1951 after a request to the War Department for the rest of my ribbons. That is when I learned that I had received the Bronze Star.

My mother had to persuade me to begin to use a fork again. I had realized in prison camp that I could really manage my food with only a spoon because I had successfully done without a fork for about two months at that time. And that's when I resolved that if I ever got home I would never use a fork again. A fork leaks. However, I finally did listen to my mother and began to learn to eat with a fork again.

The business of saying exactly what was on my mind took me a lot longer to get out of my system. I worked on my job as a forestry helper until Christmas. Then I went back to college and found out that I was rich because of the GI Bill. I didn't have to worry about how to pay my tuition or room and board and I had a few dollars a month left over for spending change. I drove my car back to school and then I sold it for $30. Soon after I got back to school, I wrote to the City of Detroit and resigned from my job as forestry helper. I believed that once I graduated, I would go back to the city, start making money, and never get into doing God's work. So I resigned from the forestry job because I said, "When I graduate, I want to be open to go wherever God calls me to go."

My brother Nelson and I were roommates on the second floor of a building that housed the college store. There were only about eighteen men in that "dorm." All of the rest of them were white, but all of us were vets. While we still could not sit at the same "civilized," American table all together in the cafeteria, we got along well together.

• • •

EPILOGUE

After graduation from Emmanuel Missionary College in June of 1948, I was called to teach at Oakwood College in Huntsville, Alabama, by Elder F. L. Peterson. That was a significant way in which God ruled in my life; my teaching career has proved to be a great and blessed privilege and a soul-satisfying occupation. I had set my sights on becoming a farmer. I graduated from EMC with a degree in agriculture. I was actually the farm manager at Oakwood College for two years but God had other plans. Nine years after graduation from EMC and a master's degree in agriculture from Michigan State College, God convinced me that teaching was my true calling. I was a science teacher in the Baltimore Public Schools at the time. I prayed to my Father in Heaven, and reasoned with Him that since every time I tried to find a job that would supply the capital to buy a farm; I ended up being a teacher. (At that time, seven years in Oakwood College and/or Oakwood Academy, one year teaching auto mechanics to soldiers at Aberdeen Proving Ground, and one year in public school in Baltimore.) I vowed in my prayer that I would teach for the rest of my life and that I would teach in God's schools for the rest of my life. My wife was the only one that knew of that prayer. About six weeks later, I received a call from The Lake Region Conference to be the science teacher at Shiloh Academy in Chicago. This continued a teaching career that lasted for forty plus more years. Shiloh Academy (Chicago), two years; Sharon Jr. Academy (Inkster, Michigan), three years; Oakwood College, fourteen more years; and Pine Forge Academy (Pine Forge, Pennsylvania) twenty-two years.

I courted a very beautiful young woman, a 1948 graduate of Oakwood College, by long distance during my first year of teaching at OC. She was teaching grades five through eight in church school in New Orleans and I made that trip five times, during that year. That was no fun riding a bus through the state of Mississippi during that year. We were married on June 26, 1949, and our firstborn son arrived on June 26, 1950. Over the next eleven years we became the parents of five more children.

We don't look particularly happy in this picture but it was 94 degrees that day. We couldn't believe that it was really happening.

This is the roster of present Smith family: Rothacker and Dorothy, Barry C. Smith, Marcia L. and *Dr. William Hicks*, Karen D. Smith, Dr. Brian and *Tammy* Smith, Candace E. C. *Williams*, Zanita G. and *Herbert Buchanan*. My father told me after Zanita had been delivered, "Son, I know that God said be fruitful and multiply and replenish the earth, but He didn't tell you to do it by yourself." Six grandchildren have been added to the family. God has blessed me throughout my sojourn on this earth and promised me a contuance in the earth made new as child of the King.

We will celebrate our 60th anniversary on June 26, 2009.

I have written this synopsis of the first half of my life to tell you how much my Jesus has done for me. I would not be here today without His saving my life may times, not only during the war but many times since those days. He has comforted and strengthened me through many trials and tribulations through the years. Two of His promises have sustained me many times: "*But he knoweth the way that I take: [when] he hath tried me, I shall come forth as gold* (Job 23:10). And "*and, lo, I am with you always, [even] unto the end of the world. Amen* (Mathew 28:20). Get to know Him as your personal Savior and

Friend and your life will be more meaningful and enjoyable than it has ever been.

I belong to that brotherhood of soldiers who have been shot at, or for Vietnam Vets, were "in country," or who have been "in harm's way." I have had opportunity to talk to members of this "brother-hood." Oftentimes our talking together brings comfort. I am willing to talk to anyone who might want the attention of a good listener.

Rothacker Smith
Docrock
docrock@knology.net

• • •

5939657R0

Made in the USA
Lexington, KY
29 June 2010